An Introduction to Latin Elegiac Verse Composition

Joseph Hirst Lupton

BIBLIOLIFE

AN INTRODUCTION

TO

LATIN ELEGIAC VERSE

COMPOSITION

BY

J. H. LUPTON, M.A.

SURMASTER OF ST PAUL'S SCHOOL,
AND FORMERLY FELLOW OF ST. JOHN'S COLLEGE, CAMBRIDGE

London

MACMILLAN AND CO.

1885

TO

THE REV. GEORGE ASH BUTTERTON, D.D.

LATE HEADMASTER OF GIGGLESWICK SCHOOL
FORMERLY FELLOW OF ST. JOHN'S COLLEGE, CAMBRIDGE

THIS LITTLE WORK

IS GRATEFULLY INSCRIBED

BY

AN OLD PUPIL

PREFACE.

THIS little work is meant to be partly introductory, partly supplementary, to the *Progressive Exercises* of Mr. Gepp. It will serve as an introduction to that deservedly popular treatise, inasmuch as it begins with the simplest elements of Latin verse composition. It may also serve as a supplement, from its containing a number of Exercises similar in form to those there given. So far as it is competent to answer this latter purpose, no apology need be made for its appearance. After a few years' use in school, even the best text-books need to have their exercises varied, or their usefulness becomes clogged by the floating mass of renderings that gradually accumulates. Should the present work prove serviceable, it would still be the author's desire to add a supplement of fresh Exercises to it after a due interval has elapsed.

At the same time, while no merit is claimed for it beyond its thus offering an additional field of choice, it has not been written without an effort to keep some-

what more closely than usual to the ancient models.
The author cannot but feel that modern Latin verse
composition is often open to severe criticism on the
ground of the laxity of rules it displays.   Far more
strictness is required in the usage of words and con-
structions.   It may be safely said that an educated
Roman of the age of Virgil or Ovid would be puzzled
to attach any meaning to many of the verses that now
pass current as elegant versions of English lines.   The
words are Latin, but the idiom is not.   Or, if he had
no difficulty with the meaning, his sense of propriety
would be offended by the incongruous tessellation of
words and phrases from authors of different periods and
styles.   The effect on him can easily be imagined, by
considering what an educated English reader would
feel, at having lines before him in which characteristic
words and turns of expression were ingeniously blended
together from Scott and Cowper, Spenser and Pope,
Dryden and Tennyson, Browning and Dr. Isaac Watts.
Even in the usage of single words, where the facts
might seem to be more easily ascertained, a culpable
laxity prevails.   To take a very few instances :—
Melos is one of the most favourite words in modern
Latin elegiacs, though no classic elegiac poet uses it,
and no Augustan poet at all, except Horace in one
passage of his *Odes*.   It was plainly felt to be a
Grecism, as the Greek form of the plural in Lucretius,

melē, shows. *Rivulus*, another favourite word, is found
in no classical poet at all. It occurs in Cicero, but
the first poet to use it is, I believe, Prudentius. *Rivus*
was itself "a rivulet," and the Roman poets did not want
the word. Another common offender is *nympha* as an
equivalent to *puella*. In its proper sense of a demi-
goddess it occurs often enough, and also in the sense of
a bride. But I am not sure whether any better
sanction for it in the sense of *puella* can be found than
Ovid, *Her. Ep.* ix. 103: "Se quoque nympha tuis
ornavit Iordanis armis," said of Omphale, the daughter
of Iordanes, King of Lydia. Even there, as she is
spoken of as the bride of Hercules, it might be a
question whether the true sense is not "thy bride,
the daughter of Iordanes," in the same way as it
is used in *Ep.* i. 27. In any case the passage is
not enough to justify the common use of the word
in the plural for "maidens." Much the same may
be said of *sinus*, freely used for "bosom" or "heart"
in the sense of the seat of the emotions. Even
in the stanza prefixed as a motto to *Arundines
Cami*, and retained in the last edition, this mis-
apprehension of its meaning is shown. It is "bosom"
indeed, but in the sense in which "he that bindeth
up the sheaves" can fill it, as Proserpine does in
Ov. *Met.* v. 393. If emotion is to be expressed, it is
denoted by the visible throbbing of the *sinus*, as in

Ep. v. 37. In like manner *ocellus* ought not to be employed as a synonym for *oculus*, being properly used of a soft, drooping eye, as that of a maiden, or the eye of a dying man. Words like *Borealis* and *scatebrosus* have no respectable authority at all; and though *lēvis* and *fragmen* are both good poetical words, what would a Roman have thought of *aequora levia* for the smooth surface of water, or of *fragmina vocis*, as a rendering of the "fragments of her mighty voice" of Tennyson? *Amplius haud* is an offender now seldom seen; but words like *almus* and *usque* are still often used with a disregard of their exact force.

Enough has, however, been said on this topic. The author does not presume to suppose that the versions used for the present work are free from fault on the above, or like, grounds. Certainly those of his own composition are not. But it is well to revise standards from time to time; and not to forget that Latin verse composition is, or ought to be, a tolerably severe exercise for the human intellect.

It will be seen that, with a view to making the Exercises as simple and easy to beginners as possible, the Latin words necessary for the first xxiv Exercises are all given on the page, and those for the next xxvi in a Vocabulary at the end. This Vocabulary was added in deference to the opinion,—on such matters always to be received with respect, of the High Master of St. Paul's, Mr. Walker. For the remaining Exercises, it has been thought that the literal retranslation and hints given with each will render them not too difficult, while at the same time the learner will have the encouraging feeling that he is translating original passages, often worth remembering for their own merits as English poetry. The Vocabulary at the end will still be found partially serviceable for these Exercises.

It now only remains for the author to thank those friends from whose assistance he has derived all that can give any value to his book.

To his old master, the Rev. G. A. Butterton, whose pen is still ready, though he has passed more than twice the eight *lustra* of the Roman poet, his thanks are due in the first instance; also to F. A. Paley, Esq., the editor of *Aeschylus*, for several excellent versions; to Mrs. Shilleto, for permission to use two copies with the familiar initials R. S., which no pupil of that scholar can ever see without lively interest; to Alfred Robinson, Esq., of New College, as executor of the late Professor John Conington, for leave, most courteously given, to use several pieces by that master of Latinity; to Henry Jackson, Esq., Fellow of Trinity; to Sir R. K. Wilson, Bart., of Newnham, for his version of the lines of Alaric Watts; to the Rev. Jackson Mason, Vicar of Settle, and formerly Scholar of Trinity; to his old pupil, J. H. Taylor, Esq., late Scholar of Trinity, for

much friendly interest in the work, as well as for
several versions; and to the friends of another old
pupil, the late Arthur W. South, also a Scholar of
Trinity, for one spirited version. He has also inserted
one piece from the unpublished translations of each of
two distinguished scholars, to whom his thanks can no
longer be paid;—the late Dr. Donaldson and the late
Dr. Kynaston. A few copies have been used, the
authors of which could not be ascertained. Should
any of these be identified, the writer trusts that he
will not have given offence by so using them. If the
Latin renderings are published in a collected form,
for the use of tutors, the initials of the translators
will be added, as far as possible. The author will
be grateful for any corrections, or suggestions of
improvement.

ST. PAUL'S SCHOOL,
    Aug. 1, 1885.

PART I.

INTRODUCTION.

§ 1. RHYTHM AND METRE.

To be a good versifier, as to be a good musician, requires not only practice, but also the possession of certain natural gifts. One of the chief of these, though at the same time one which may be largely improved by cultivation, is the faculty known as a good ear for sound. In versemaking it should be an object to develope this faculty as much as possible. To construct verses by the eye, by grouping words together in the order of a particular pattern, is an exercise as profitless as it is uninteresting. The learner should make an effort, from the first, to hear mentally, if not audibly, the sound of the verses he is composing; and to learn to depend on the ear for guidance as to what is right and what is wrong.

With this view, it will be of service to him to try to gain at the outset some true conception of *rhythm*, or measured sequence of sounds, and *metre*, or the application of rhythmical laws to words. Listen to the steady beat of a blacksmith's hammer on the anvil. We may say that the measure there is by ones. There is no difference between any two consecutive strokes. But notice now the change of sound when, as sometimes happens, the hammer is allowed to drop on the anvil after each blow. The sounds then reach our ears in pairs, the first of each being louder and sharper (though not lasting longer) than the second. Something of the same effect is observable in the trotting of a horse. The sounds again come in pairs, though the second of each may be more nearly equal to the first than in the case just mentioned. Once more, listen to the beat of a horse's feet when cantering. The sounds then come in triplets, or sets of three, the first of each set being more sharply marked than the other two.

As all human speech is more or less rhythmical, it is easy to produce any of these effects of sound by arranging words so that the accents come in the required order. To take a familiar example from Tennyson's *Northern Farmer*, any ear could recognise what was meant to be imitated in the line ;—

But proputty proputty sticks, an' proputty proputty graws.

Two observations have to be made before we come to consider any of the Greek or Latin metres. One is, that the natural character of a language makes it better adapted for some metres than for others ; and the other, that while in Greek and Latin, metre was determined by what is called *quantity*, in English, as in other modern languages, it is so by what we call accent.[1]

The English is naturally an iambic speech ; that is, the sequence of accented syllables is such that it falls most

---

[1] This can be best illustrated by the use of musical notation, as is done by Wilhelm Christ, in his *Metrik der Griechen und Römer* (1879), pp. 220 *sqq.* ; but brevity must here be studied.

readily into the metrical order in which a light or un-accented syllable is followed by one more strongly marked. The notation for an *iambus* is ⌣ —. A proof of this, if any were needed, is the ease with which whole passages of good prose can be arranged in what is called blank verse.[1] But in the Latin dactylic metre, with which alone this book is concerned, the rhythm is of a kind in which the longer, or more emphasized, syllable, comes first. Hence we shall be prepared to find that English does not adapt itself readily to the true dactylic metre. This becomes still more evident when the other consideration just men-tioned is taken count of. That is, that while the Latin measure is determined by *quantity*, the English is so by accent. In triple time in music, the three notes to each beat are of equal length; only one, generally the first, is accentuated. If the three notes were (say) a crotchet and two quavers to each beat, that would not be triple time at all. Now, an English *dactyl* answers to the former of these, and might be denoted by ⌣ ⌣ ⌣. The Latin dactyl answered to the latter, and its notation is — ⌣ ⌣.

Take a few examples, such as Coleridge's imitative line:—

In the hex|ameter | rises the | fountain's | silvery | column ,

Or Longfellow's :—

Softly the | Angelus | sounded, and | over the | roofs of the | village ;

Or the dactylic lines of Hood :—

> Over the | brink of it,
> Picture it, | think of it,
> Dissolute | man.

---

[1] See, for an instance, *Cambridge Essays* (1855), p. 177 n., where passages from Dickens are so arranged

and compare them with any ordinary Virgilian line, such
as this one, answering in form to Coleridge's :—

    Praeteri|tae veni|am·dabit | igno|rantia | culpae ;

and the difference will be apparent. The Latin is properly
recited to a time of two beats to each bar or division
(called in metrical language *feet*) ; while the English goes
more naturally to triple time, in which the three syllables
of each bar, or foot, answer to one beat, with an accentua-
tion of the first. One reason is that, while the syllables
in Latin are nearly phonetic, in English the vowels are
clogged by consonants, so that even such heavy monosyllables as " should'st " may have to be counted as un-
accented syllables, as in the line

    And thoú | should'st smíle | no móre |.

§ 2. The Elegiac Metre.

This metre, the μέτρον ἐλεγεῖον of the Greeks, the one
in which Ovid excelled,[1] and which is thought most easy
of imitation for beginners, is formed by two lines of unequal length recurring alternately. The first line of every
couplet is called a *hexameter* (ἕξ, μέτρον), as consisting of six
metres, in the restricted sense of the word *metre*, or feet.
The second, or shorter, line, in like manner is called a
pentameter (πέντε, μέτρον) from an assumption that it con-

---

[1] The inimitable flexibility, as well as finish, displayed by Ovid in
the somewhat confining limits of this metre, makes it doubly to be
regretted that his choice of subjects is such that we turn with relief to
Virgil. Hence arises the practical inconvenience, to be met with in
many schools, that while a boy's composition is in elegiacs, his reading
is in Virgilian hexameters.

sisted of five feet. This will be presently seen to be not quite correct.

What the hexameter is, will have been partly seen above. It is essentially dactylic; that is, its proper feet are dactyls, relieved here and there by spondees, not conversely. Agreeably with this, taking the Homeric line as the original type, we find a *trochee* (– ◡) in the last place more frequently than a spondee. Hence the sounder theory which regards it as a " dactylic hexameter *catalectic* " (that is, ending before the full measure of feet is completed), rather than as *acatalectic* or complete.[1] But in the more stately Latin a spondee is preferred for the last foot, though the trochee (– ◡), or curtailed dactyl, is not unfrequent.

The pentameter took its name from a theory of some old grammarians [2] that it consisted of five *metres*, or feet, scanned regularly on, as – ◡‾◡ | – ◡‾◡ | – – | ◡ ◡ – | ◡ ◡ ≚. But it is much more correct to say that it is formed of two incomplete dactylic trimeters; the first being of this form :

$$- \overline{\smile\smile} \,|\, - \overline{\smile\smile} \,|\, -$$

and the second of this :—

$$- \smile \smile \,|\, - \smile \smile \,|\, \simeq$$

For the present it will be enough to say that the hexameter, or first line of every couplet, consists of six feet, of which any of the first four may be either a dactyl or a spondee, while the fifth must be a dactyl, and the sixth a

[1] See Dr. Kennedy's *Public School Latin Grammar* (1883), p. 526.

[2] Quintilian (ix. 4. 98) and Terentianus Maurus, quoted by Wilhelm Christ, as above, p. 207. See also Donaldson's *Latin Grammar* (1850), p. 447.

spondee or a trochee; and that the pentameter, or second line, consists of two *penthemimers* (or half hexameters), admitting a dactyl or a spondee indifferently as the complete feet of the first half, but only two dactyls as those of the second. The third, or incomplete foot of the first half, must be a long syllable; that of the second half may be either long or short, though a long one is preferred.

The complete scale of feet for the elegiac couplet is :—

$$- \smile \bar{\smile} \mid - \smile \bar{\smile} \mid - \smile \bar{\smile} \mid - \smile \bar{\smile} \mid - \smile \smile \mid - \bar{\smile}$$
$$- \smile \bar{\smile} \mid - \smile \bar{\smile} \mid \quad - \quad \| - \smile \smile \mid - \smile \smile \mid \smile$$

The simple reason of what may seem to the beginner as a rather bewildering arrangement of "incomplete" feet, is probably to be found in the fact that the ear requires pauses in sound, in order to be gratified. An unbroken succession of dactyls would be monotonous and wearisome.

Many other rules will have to be attended to, in composing entire verses in this metre, especially one about the *cæsura*, or division of the hexameter at certain points. But these will be most wisely reserved till afterwards. His best course at this stage, instead of burdening his memory with rules, will be to commit to memory as many well-chosen passages of Ovid as he can; such as

> Unda repercussae radiabat imagine lunae,
> Et nitor in tacita nocte diurnus erat:
> Nullaque vox usquam, nullum veniebat ad aures
> Praeter dimotae corpore murmur aquae.

He will thus acquire a perception of the laws of the metre from catching the sound of it in its purest forms, and can verify his impressions by rules later on. Meanwhile let him begin with portions of a line, as in the ensuing exercises, and gradually extend his range.

EXERCISE I.

$$- \smile \smile \mid - \smile$$

Mārmŏră | pōntī
Flūmĭnĭs | ūndă

On the model of the above, write in Latin—

1.	An island of the sea	insula pontus.
2.	The shores of the land	litus terra.
3.	He breaks the treaties	foedus rumpo.
4.	I will leave the pastures	linquo pascuum.
5.	Greece has conquered	Graecia vinco.
6.	A shadow of a name	umbra nomen.
7.	The cold of winter	frigus (*pl.*) bruma.
8.	Jupiter dares	Jupiter audeo.
9.	The rising of the light	ortus lumen.
10.	With murmur of rivulet	murmur rivus.
11.	Times of mourning	tempus luctus.
12.	Iron weapons	ferreus telum.
13.	Gifts of right-hand	munus dextra.
14.	He betrays crimes	prodo crimen.
15.	By the weight of the stone	pondus saxum.
16.	Thou beholdest a temple	aspicio aedes.
17.	He had sent gold	mitto aurum.
18.	The hero had lived	heros vivo.
19.	The stars of night	sidus nox.
20.	He will destroy citadels	diruo arx.

EXERCISE II.

$$- \smile \smile \mid - \;\breve{}$$

Sōlă vŏ|lūptās
Crēdĭt ă|māntĭ
Vĭtĭs ĭn | ārvō

1. Gifts of the maiden	donum puella.
2. He himself will favour	ipse faveo.
3. The enemy was departing	hostis abeo.
4. They seem hard things	videor durus.
5. Weapons will shine	telum niteo.
6. Discharge arrows	mitto sagitta.
7. The use of the plough	usus aratrum.
8. Orders of parents	jussum parens.
9. If any one shall approach	siquis adeo.
10. Whoever was entering	quisquis ineo.
11. Thou wilt fear arms	timeo arma (*n. pl.*)
12. By love of praise	amor laus.
13. The gate was falling	porta ruo.
14. Thou wilt often ask	saepe rogo.
15. Greater than Homer	magnus Homerus (*ab*
16. A tree in hot-weather	arbor in aestus.
17. He scatters on the fields	spargo in ager.
18. In the hours of the night	in hora nox.
19. He goes-on towards the river	pergo ad amnis.
20. Learn by teaching	disco doceo (*ger.*)

EXERCISE III.

$$\smile \; \underline{\smile} \; | \; - \; \smile \; \smile \; | \; - \; \underline{\smile}$$

Dē|gēntĕ vĭ|rōrūm
Sīl|vāquĕ rĕ|cōndĭt
Prŏcŭl | ēstĕ, prŏ|fānī

1. From the race of the gods	de stirps deus.
2. Thee, O son, shall I leave	tu, natus, relinquo.
3. To hope-for safety	spero salus.
4. He recognised friends	agnosco amicus.
5. Thus speaking with voice	sic loquor (*pf. ptcp.*)
	vox.
6. Now drive ye back	nunc pello retro.
7. Rescued from the waves	eripio ab unda.
8. I learn to succour	disco succurro.
9. And hung on his neck	pendeoque collum.
10. And tables removed	mensaque removeo
	(*pf. ptcp.*)
11. To the guardians of the citadel	custos arx.
12. He hurls against the walls	torqueo in moenia.
13. Far-off behold a tower	procul aspicio turris.
14. Fear added wings	timor addo ala.
15. New realms are sought	novus regnum peto.
16. From the origin of the race	ab origo gens.
17. To the city of his sire	ad urbs genitor.
18. And with blood-stained hands	cruentus que manus.
19. Four times the arms were sounding	quater arma sono.
20. The broad waters shine-again	latus fretum reluceo.

EXERCISE IV.

HITHERTO there has been little or no need to call to mind the rules of prosody, because the words given could only be arranged in one way. But as the number of feet increases, the learner must be able to discern at a glance what the quantity of each syllable is, that he may not lose time in trying wrong arrangements of the words. A few helps only can be given here. For further aid, the chapter on Prosody in the Latin Grammar must be studied. The best preparation of all, however, will be found to consist in committing to memory choice passages of Ovid, or good versions of favourite English pieces, and maintaining, as far as possible, a consistent pronunciation of long vowels as long, and of short ones as short. If the common English way of pronouncing Latin is retained, preserve the length of long vowels as you would in case of similar English words. Thus, *scrĭbĕrĕ* should be read with the first syllable as in *scribe*, not as in *scribble*. On the other hand, *bŏnus* should not be read as *bone us*. If one pronounces *etiam* as *eeshyam*, both the quantity and the etymology are needlessly disguised. In short, as said before, learn to trust the ear rather than the eye. This being premised, the following general rules will be found useful :—

1. Many vowels are long or short *by nature*, as the expression is ; that is, we find them to be so as a matter of fact in the poets. *Why* these are so is a question at present beyond us. If we find the first two syllables of *sĕrēnus*, for example, scanned as *serene* is in English,

we must accept it as a fact; and for this and multitudes of other words we shall have to depend on memory.

2. If we perceive that a vowel is the result of the contraction of two vowels, or of two syllables, into one, as *tūtus* from *tŭĭtus*, *mōbilis* from *mŏvĭbilis*, we shall know that it is long. Hence diphthongs as a rule are long.

3. If a vowel is followed by another, the two being in different syllables, and not combining in a diphthong, the former is generally short, as *rŭam*, *pĭŭs*. Except genitives and datives singular of the fifth declension, with nominatives in -*es* pure, as *diēi ;* also genitives in -*ius*, as *illīus* (*alīus* always long, *alterĭus* always short); also the *i* in *fĭo*, in all parts of the verb where it is not followed by -*er*.

4. If a vowel stands before two consonants, as in *pārtibus*, *ēt tibi*, it is made long by its position, though it may be naturally short. The exception is when the two consonants are a mute followed by a liquid, not divided between two syllables, as *patrem*, *tenebras*, *volucres ;* but *ŏbruo*, because the *b* and *r* are in different syllables. It will be observed that the liquid in each of these words is *r*, and combinations of *br*, *cr*, *pr*, *tr*, are in practice all that you will have to attend to.

Before these combinations a vowel, if naturally short, may remain short, or it may be scanned long at pleasure. If naturally long, it is of course not made common by being so placed. Thus, *mātrem* never would have the *a* short, any more than *māter*.

5. If a word ends in a short vowel, it is not affected by the next word's beginning with two consonants. Thus,

ventiqué fremebant is as correct as *ventiqué sonabant.* But
if the initial consonants be *sc*, *sp*, *sq*, *st*, or the double
letters *x* or *z*, the preceding final vowel is not allowed
to be scanned short. As, moreover, the examples of
its being made long by such a position, if naturally
short, as in *occultâ spolia et plures de pace triumphos*, are
few and in some cases doubtful, the practical rule is
to avoid altogether the placing of a short vowel before
any one of those combinations of letters.

6. The letter *h* does not count as a consonant.

7. If a word ends in a vowel or the letter *m*, and the next
word begins with a vowel or the letter *h*, the former
suffers elision. Thus in the lines—

> Conticuere‿omnes, intentique‿ora tenebant
> Disce, puer, virtutem‿ex me verumque laborem,

the syllables *-re* and *que* in the former, and *-em* in the
latter, are so lightly pronounced that they do not
count in the scanning. The feet are the same as if
the poet had written *conticuēr' omnes, virtūt' ex me*, and
so on. In Greek the final vowel is in fact omitted
when an elision takes place; but it is a mistake in
reading Latin to treat these terminations as altogether
absent. The *-em* in *virtutem*, for example, having
probably only a faint nasal sound, could easily be
ignored in scansion, but in recitation it should still be
lightly sounded.[1] The principle will be better understood by noticing the rapid liaisons of vowels in
spoken Italian, or the final nasal sounds in French.

[1] See Harkness's *Latin Grammar*, p. 353, note. In schools this rule
is very commonly neglected.

8. The rules for the quantity of final vowels are subject to
so many exceptions that only the most general state-
ments can here be made.   Allowing for this, we may
arrange them as follows :—

VOWEL ENDINGS.

Short.

-*ă*. The nominative and vocative singular of nouns of
the first declension, as
mensă, and corresponding
adjective forms, as *iniquă*,
all neuter plurals in -*a*, as
regnă, mariă, turbidă ; and
some indeclinable words,
as *ită* and *quiă*.

-*ĕ*. Every nominative and
vocative singular in -*e*,
whether noun or adject-
tive, as *Turnĕ, marĕ, tristĕ* ;
all ablatives in -*e*, as *nubĕ*,
operĕ, meliorĕ, excepting of
the fifth declension, as
diĕ, and *famĕ* of the third ;
all parts of verbs in -*e*, as
regĕ, audirĕ, excepting the
2d person singular imperative active of the second
conjugation, as *monĕ* ; the
adverbs *benĕ, malĕ* ; the en-
clitics, -*nĕ*, -*quĕ*, and some
others.

Long.

-*ā*. The ablative singular of
nouns of the first declension, as *mensā*, and corresponding adjective forms,
as *iniquā* ; the 2d person
present imperative active
of the first conjugation, as
amā ; and some indeclinable words, as *contrā*,
frustrā, intereā, posteā.

-*ē*. The ablative singular of all
nouns of the fifth declension, as *spē, diē* ; the 2d
person singular present
imperative active of
the second conjugation,
as *vidē, monē* ; adverbs in -*e*
from adjectives of three
terminations, as *rectē, clarē* ;
the prohibitive particle *nē*.

Short.

-*ĭ.* A few indeclinable words, as *nisĭ, quasĭ,* and compounds of *ubi* in which it comes last, as *sicubĭ.* In *mihĭ, tibĭ, sibĭ, ubĭ, ibĭ,* the *i* is common.

-*ŏ.* The pronoun *egŏ ; homŏ* (though *homō* in Lucretius, Catullus and Hor. *Sat.* i. 2, 31) ; the numerals *duŏ, octŏ ;* the verbs *sciŏ, nesciŏ, putŏ ;* and the adverbs *ciŏ, modŏ.*

Long.

-*ī.* All noun - endings, as *dominī, nostrī ,* all verb-endings, as *audī, vertī ,* and the conjunctions *nī* and *sī.* Their compound *nisĭ* has both vowels short.

-*ō.* All datives and ablatives singular, as *puerō, nitidō, vigilandō ,* and most adverbs, as *adeō, ergō* (nearly always), *quandō,* etc.

Post-Augustan poets sometimes shorten the -*ŏ* in nouns of the third declension like *virgo,* and in the 1st person present indicative of verbs, as *scando ;* but the beginner should avoid this licence.

-*ŭ.* Practically, none. This letter must not be confounded with the Greek *υ (upsilon),* which is, as its name implies, naturally short. The Greek *upsilon* is expressed in Latin by -*y,* and this is short, as in *Tiphў, Molў.*

-*ū.* In all words, as *genū, diū.*

CONSONANTAL ENDINGS.

Short.	*Long.*

-b. In monosyllables, as *ăb*, *ŏb*.

-b. In none.

-c. In *nĕc* and *dōnĕc.*
In *hic* (nom. pron.) the *i* is common, though more often long than short.

-c. In *hoc* (pronoun), whether nominative, accusative, or ablative; in adverbs, as *hic*, *illic*, *sic.*

-d. In all words, as *ăd*, *illŭd.*

-d. In none.

-l. In nearly all words, as *mĕl*, *semĕl*, *nihĭl*, *procŭl*, *Hannibăl.*

-l. In *nīl* (contracted from *nihil*), and *sōl.*

-n. In all nouns, except a few monosyllabic or Greek nouns, as *nōmĕn*, *flūmĕn ;* and in indeclinable words, as *ĭn*, *tamĕn*, *forsĭtăn.*

-n. In a few monosyllables, as *nōn*, *sīn*, *quīn* (all being contractions), and *ēn* ($= \check{\eta}\nu$).

-r. In all words not of Greek origin, except a few monosyllables, as *calcăr*, *itĕr*, *audiŏr*, *trudŭntŭr.* The short monosyllables are *fĕr*, *pĕr*, *tĕr*, *vĭr*, and *cŏr.*

-r. In nouns of the third declension in *-er*, increasing in the genitive, as *āĕr*, *aethĕr*, *vēr* (all of Greek origin) ; those not so increasing being short, as *patĕr*, *matĕr.* Long monosyllables are *păr* and *fūr.*

C

Short.

-*ăs.* Only in words borrowed from the Greek, as *Arcăs, hērŏăs. Anăs,* a duck, is found, but not in any good poet.

-*ĕs.* In the nominative and vocative singular of nouns of the third declension increasing with penult short in the genitive, as *hospĕs, -ĭtis, pedĕs, -ĭtis* (except *pĕs,* with its compounds, as *sonipĕs,* and *abiĕs, ariĕs, Cerĕs, pariĕs*); also *ĕs* from *sum,* and its compounds, as *abĕs, potĕs ;* and the preposition *penĕs.*

.

-*ĭs.* In the nominative and genitive singular of all nouns of the third declension, as *ensĭs, rēgĭs,* including adjectives and pronouns, as *mollĭs, ĭs, quĭs,* but excepting one or two monosyllables, as *vĭs ;* in all verb terminations except those mentioned opposite, as

Long.

-*ās.* In all strictly Latin words, as *nautās, certās, ās, crās.*

-*ēs.* In the nominative and accusative plural of all nouns of the third and fifth declension, as *dŭcēs, peditēs ;* in nominatives singular of that declension increasing with long penult in the genitive, as *locuplēs, -ĕtis ;* in all verb endings, as *dūcēs, rĕmŏvēs.* Account is not taken of Greek nouns such as *Anchisēs, lampadēs,* which follow the quantity of their original vowels.

-*īs.* In all datives and ablatives plural, as *terrīs, nobīs ,* in the second person singular present indicative of verbs of the fourth conjugation, as *audīs ;* in the same person of every present subjunctive in -*is,* as *sīs, velīs, possīs ,* in *fīs,* and in *vīs*

Short.

cernĭs, rĕgĭs, terrĕbĭs, possĭtĭs ; and in the indeclinables bĭs and magĭs.

The termination -rĭs in the 2d person singular perfect subjunctive and future perfect of verbs, as amaveris, feceris, is common.

-ŏs. Neglecting words of Greek origin, as Tethyŏs, only in ŏs, a bone, and its compound exŏs, and in compŏs.

-ŭs. In all noun terminations, except those mentioned opposite, as servŭs, tempŭs, iniquŭs, solĭbŭs, quibŭs ; in all verb terminations, as findimŭs ; and in all indeclinable words, as intŭs, rursŭs.

Long.

and its compounds, from vŏlo ; in the accusative plural of nouns of the third declension, representing -eis, as civĭs, omnĭs ; and in some indeclinable words, as forĭs, gratĭs.

-ōs. In all accusatives plural of the second declension, including adjectival and pronominal forms, as ventōs, aliquōs, hōs, vōs ; in the nominative singular of all nouns of the third declension in -os, increasing with long penult in the genitive, as ōs (a mouth), custōs, honōs.

-ūs. In the nominative singular of nouns in -us of the third declension, increasing with long penult in the genitive, as rūs, virtūs, tellūs ; and in the genitive singular, and nominative, vocative, and accusative plural of nouns of the fourth declension, as luctūs, arcūs.

EXERCISE V.[1]

$$- \left| \begin{array}{cc} - & - \\ - & \smile \smile \end{array} \right| - \smile \smile \left| - \overset{\smile}{-} \right.$$

Plūs|quām fā|cūndŭs Ŭ|līxēs.
Cūm | crāstĭnă | fūlsĕrĭt | hōră.

1. Following the guiding threads	secutus ducens filum.
2. Twice five talents of gold	bis quinque talentum aurum.
3. It is not safe to despise	non est tutus contemno.
4. To-be-regained by no art	ars nullus reparabilis.
5. Hurling spear with arm	lacertus hastile torqueo.
6. The elm is clasped by vines	ulmus vincior vitis.
7. Whelm ye the bark in the sea	demergo puppis pontus.
8. He is not to-be-cured by simples	non medicabilis herba est.
9. Destroyed by civil war	perimo mars civilis.
10. And more fickle than breeze of-spring	incertior que aura verna.
11. Mother of beautiful Iulus	formosus Ĩulus mater.
12. Perjuries of false tongue	perjurium falsa lingua.
13. Child of a pitiable mother	infans miserabilis mater.
14. May he fill the years happily	impleo annus feliciter.
15. A city as great as Carthage	urbs (acc.) instar Carthago (gen.)

---

[1] In this and the following Exercises the Latin words are given, as a rule, in the order of the English. In placing them as required for the metre, remember that the enclitic *que* should follow the first word.

16. And the shepherd was driving   pastor que ago armen-
    herds   tum.

17. Let the waters grow white   aequor cănesco remus.
    with oars

18. Fortune urges pertinaciously   fortuna urgeo tenaciter.

19. Aim-at his body with drawn   peto corpus (*pl.*) strictus
    sword   ferrum.

20. Thou wilt give sails to winds carbasus   (*neut.   pl.*)
                                   ventus praebeo.

21. Thou hast seen the eyes of a   video ocellus fleo (*pres.*
    weeper   *ptcp.*)

22. Let us be numbered in that   numero in ista turba.
    throng

23. What Priam himself may ad-   quid   ipse   Priamus
    vise   suadeo.

24. But evil destiny (*pl.*) was sed fatum malum ego
    drawing me   traho.

EXERCISE VI.

$$\smile\smile \mid \frac{--}{-\smile\smile} \mid -\smile\smile \mid -\,\overset{\smile}{-}$$

Lăcrĭ|māe fē|cērĕ lĭ|tūrās
Quĭd ĕ|nĭm vĕrĕ|ārĭs, ĭn|ĭquĕ ?

1. To hurl the javelin with his   vibro jaculum lacertus.
   arm

2. Would that thou wert change-   utinam sum (*imp. subj.*)
   able   mutabilis.

3. The herds from stalls set open — armentum stabulum recludo.

4. On a sudden he arrived at the cities — subito ad urbs pervenio.

5. Because I am called the wife of Hercules — quia Hercules uxor nomino.

6. Anger befits the tragic buskin — ira deceo cothurnus tragicus.

7. He will pass to other lands — transeo in alius ager.

8. The steers are coming to the ploughs — juvencus venio ad aratrum.

9. The sister of the Thunderer would desire this — germana Tonans hic volo (*pres. subj.*)

10. And Aegisthus with throat cut-open — Aegisthus que apertum jugulum.

11. One home pleased the two — unus domus placeo duo.

12. I will break the treaties of-alliance. — rumpo foedus socialis.

13. What harm will a long letter do ? — quid noceo longus epistola ?

14. We rested, sheltered by a tree — requiesco tego arbor.

15. Sails receding from the view (*lit.* eyes) — velum abeo oculus.

16. Agamemnon repents of his anger — paenitet Agamemnon (*acc.* -ŏnă) ira.

17. By a sudden yawning of the earth — subitus hiatus tellus.

18. And hitherto I have lived without blame — et vivo adhuc sine crimen.

19. And in the vales of lofty Ida — et in vallis alta Īda.

20. A space longer to me than a year — spatium longus ego annus.

21. And the shores become nearer — litus que fio propior.

22. No mean reward of toil — non vilis pretium labor.

23. At-times we pray with timid voice — modŏ precor vox timidus.

24. For who will depart at-ease ? — quis enim abeo securus ?

EXERCISE VII.

In this Exercise various endings of hexameter lines are given, of all the lengths separately practised in the preceding Exercises.

1. Life will remain — vita maneo.

2. And on the calends of January — kălendaeque Jănus.

3. Apply your minds — mens adverto.

4. The sea itself with its waves — aequor ipse cum fluctus.

5. Nor let the moon be light for thee — nec Phoebē sum lucidus tu.

6. The soft pasturage of the plain — molle pabulum (*pl.*) campus.

7. Gliding away into empty air — dilabor (*pf. ptcp.*) in vacuus aura.

8. I shall be tossed shipwrecked in the billows — jacto naufragus unda.

9. The birds will tear my limbs — volŭcres carpo meus membrum.

10. In the shades of night   in umbra nox.
11. Endlessly blessed   beatus sine finis.
12. They bathed in the waters of-   lavo¹ unda lacustris.
    the-pool
13. The nurse's foster-child   nutrix alumnus.
14. He was lying on the bare   jaceo nudus tellus.
    earth
15. We have aroused thy anger   moveo ira tu.
    (*lit.* anger to thee)
16. He received the sceptre from   capio sceptrum ab ille.
    him
17. The fifth from Hercules   quintus ab Hercules.
18. May their bones rest more   os quiesco feliciter.
    happily
19. Sewn up in the skin of a   insuo pellis juvenca.
    heifer
20. More modest than he   pudicus ille.
21. And Charybdis opposite to   Chărybdis que adver-
    Scylla   sus Scylla.
22. Forsaken on Aetna   desero in Aetna.
23. To change forms   muto figura.
24. You may be sacrificed at the   macto ad sacer ara.
    sacred altars

¹ Remember that the third person plural of the perfect indicative
active has two forms, in -ērunt and -ērĕ.

EXERCISE VIII.

ON THE CÆSURA.

THE portions of lines formed in Exercises V. and VI. make up the latter halves of ordinary hexameters; or, to speak more precisely, all that comes after a certain division of the line known as the *cæsura*.   Take for example such lines as—

> Verba puellarum | foliis leviora caducis
> Aut mare prospiciens | odioso concita vento.

The ear detects a certain rest, or pause, where the mark of division is placed, independent of any pause in the sense. If there were no such break, the line might satisfy all conditions as to the metrical feet composing it, and yet would be felt to be inharmonious.   Thus the opening words of Tacitus's *Annals*—

> Urbem Romam principio reges habuere,

contain the required feet, but it is plain that they do not form a true hexameter verse.   The wavy motion of a real hexameter is wanting; there is no cadence.   Or take Horace's well-known line, expressive of the ceaseless flow of a river :—

> Labitur et labetur in omne volubilis aevum.

Beautiful as it is for its purpose, and having a slight cæsural effect from the emphasis on the *e* in *labetur* (in antithesis to *labitur*), any one can feel that a succession of such lines would be monotonous and wearisome.   It would

be like a continual going down hill.   Hence the beginner
may understand something of the necessity for a kind of
pause or break near the middle of the line.   Moreover, as
the first syllable of a foot is that on which the stress of the
voice is laid, he will see the reason of the break occurring
after that syllable.   And thus we are prepared for the rule,
that *the third foot must be so divided that its first syllable shall
end a word; or, if not the third, that then the fourth foot must be
so divided.*   This division is called *cæsura,* literally, *a cutting.*
The former of the two kinds is much the commoner.   As in
the one case the division would occur at the end of the fifth
half foot, it is often described by the clumsy but convenient
name of the *penthemimeral* cæsura, from the Greek πέντε,
ἥμι-, μέρος.   In like manner the other is called the *hephthemimeral* cæsura.   Where this latter is used, there is commonly a division of the second foot in a similar manner, so
that the third half foot will also be the end of a word.   It
is no unusual thing for all three cæsuras to be found in one
and the same line, as—

Utque fugam | capiant, | aries | nitidissimus auro.

But in such cases the penthemimeral is the one to be taken
count of.   Using for the present only the first and commoner kind, let the learner compose the following parts of
lines, containing the first two and a half feet, or as far as
to the cæsura.   It will be noticed afterwards that they
are identical with the first half of a pentameter line.

EXERCISE IX.

$-\;\smile\;\smile\;|\;-\;\smile\;\smile\;|\;-$ Nēc gălĕ|ā tĕgȳ|mur.

$-\;\smile\;\smile\;|\;-\;-\;|\;-$ Vīsă sŭb | ōbscū|rum.

$-\;-\;|\;-\;\smile\;\smile\;|\;-$ Armō|rūm sŏnȳ|tum.

$-\;-\;|\;-\;-\;|\;-$ Dēbē|mūr mōr|ti.

1. They traverse every land	lustro omnis sŏlum.
2. You will there find	invenio illic.
3. They sing the arms of Caesar	cano arma Caesar.
4. He appointed months	consisto mensis.
5. Yet there is a reason also	et tamen ratio sum.
6. Hail! festal day	dies (*fem.*) festus salve.
7. He holding a staff	ille baculus teneo.
8. Learn, laying aside fear	disco, metus pono (*abl. abs.*)
9. He would have cast seeds	semen jacio.
10. They were the bulls of Mars	taurus sum Mars.
11. By the gods-above I pray	oro per superi.
12. He had come, as the story is	venio ut fama sum.
13. If you have a care for me	si tu cura ego.
14. As by a gentle breeze	ut zephyrus lenis.
15. They have shaken off fear	metus excutio.
16. I will not say what is false	non ego loquor falsus (*n. pl.*)
17. What have I to do with the sword ?	quid ego (*dat.*) cum ferrum ?
18. But neither gloomy winter	sed neque hiems tristis.
19. I am in doubt what to do	dubito quis facio (*pres. subj.*)
20. Or else we shall be foolish	aut sum stultus.

EXERCISE X.

HEPHTHEMIMERAL CÆSURA.

Ūtquĕ fă|vēt Cȳthĕ|rĕă tĭ|bi
Fēlĭ|cēs quĭbŭs | ūsŭs ăd|est
Aūt ēs|sēs fōr|mōsă mĭ|nus
Hĭc tēm|plūm Jū|nōni ĭn|gens.

As was said before, this cæsura is much less common than the penthemimeral, and is used by Ovid, in his elegiac verse, less frequently than by Virgil. For example, in the first book of the *Aeneid*, out of 756 lines, there are between 60 and 70 clear instances of it, without reckoning a considerable number of lines such as—

> Insequitur clamorque virum, stridorque rudentum
> Cymothoe simul et Triton adnixus acuto
> Servitio premet ac victis dominabitur Argis,

in which, though the fifth half foot is the last syllable of a word, yet either the addition of an enclitic, as *que*, *ve*, or the fact of that syllable being a connecting particle like *et*, *ac*, makes the true cæsura to be the hephthemimeral. In Ovid, on the other hand, if we take the last four *Epistolae* in the *Heroides* (xvi.-xix. in Riese's edition), out of 938 lines, of which, of course, only half are hexameters, there are only nine clear instances of the hephthemimeral cæsura, and the

same number of lines of the form given above.   Hence the
learner will be prepared to look on this kind of cæsura as
only an occasional variety, to relieve the monotony of the
other.

He will also note that while, in the scale given above,
any of the first three feet may be spondees, it is very rarely
found that all three are so.

1. Meantime while they deny all   interea dum nego cunc-
    things   tus.

2. These in truth and more they   hic (*fem. pl.*) certe cano
    sing   pluresque.

3. Call back your courage, my   revoco animus, o comes.
    comrades

4. Thou rulest with everlasting   rego aeternum imperi-
    sway   um.

5. A mighty war will he wage   gero bellum ingens Itălia.
    in Italy

6. I have given sovereignty   do imperium sine finis.
    without end

7 As soon as ever kindly light   ut primum almus lux
    is given   do.

8. His goddess mother showing   dea mater monstro (*abl.
    the way   abs*) via.

9. And compassed the sky with   et cingo (*pft. in* -ĕre)
    their throng   polus coetus.

10. She herself soaring-on-high   ipse sublimis abeo Pă-
    departs to Paphus   phus (*acc.*)

11. And now they were climb-   jamque collis ascendo
    ing the hill

12. Aeneas marvels-at the pile   Aeneas miror moles.

13. Like as bees in early summer qualis apis novus aestas.

14. Their work beneath the sun   labor sub sol exerceo.
    harasses
15. And turns aside his eager   averto que equus ardens.
    steeds
16. And to fit timbers in the   et apto trabs silva.
    woods
17. And of which I was a great   et qui sum magnus
    part   pars.
18. Then father Aeneas from his   inde pater Aeneas torus.
    couch
19. Now only a bay and road-   nunc sinus tantum et
    stead   statio.
20. And to see the spots forsaken   locus que video desertus.
21. And they marvel at the   et miror equus moles.
    horse's bulk
22. To terrify with fresh charges   novus crimen terreo.
23. For twice five days he is   ille sileo bis quinus dies.
    silent
24. And now the dreadful day   jamque adsum dies (*fem.*)
    was at hand   infandus.
25. I lay hid, till they should set   delitesco dum do velum
    sail   (*pl.*)

EXERCISE XI.

HAVING composed the separate sections of a hexameter
line, the learner may now begin to frame the whole.   He
will find it well to provide first for the last two feet, which
are invariable, and then to consider how the cæsura will

best fall. In the present exercise the cæsura will be uniformly the penthemimeral ; every line will begin with a dactyl ; and there will be no elisions.

1. To these mountains the whole world is one day promised.

   Totus orbis hic mons olim promitto.

2. But still all are celebrated with human honours.

   Sed tamen omnis celebro humanus honor.

3. Let the soldier bear arms alone with which to keep arms in check.

   Miles gero arma solus (*neut. pl.*) qui coerceo (*pres. subj.*) arma.

4. I am neither covered with helmet nor girt with sharp sword.

   Nec tego (*pl.*) galea nec cingo (*pl.*) acutus ensis.

5. (The month) which follows Janus was the last of the old year.

   Qui sequor Janus sum ultimus vetus annus.

6. Often has the wolf, pursuing a lamb, been kept back by (his) voice.

   Saepe lupus sequor agna retineo[1] a vox.

7. Perhaps, unhappy one, thou didst fear the winds and wave.

   Forsitan ventus undaque timeo, infelix.

8. He had put on a mantle double-dyed in Tyrian purple.

   Induo palla bis tingo Tyrius mūrex.

9. On the Ides the altars of rustic Faunus smoke.

   Īdus (*pl.*) altare agrestis Faunus fumo.

---

[1] It is not necessary that the two parts of the perfect indicative passive should stand together. In this case, the *est* may come before *retentus* and be separated from it, if required, by other words.

10. There was a plain : hills shut-in the furthest-parts of the plain.

Campus sum : collis ultimus (*neut. pl.*) campus claudo.

11. Lo ! like a torrent swollen with floods of-rain.

Ecce velut torrens augeo unda pluvialis.

12. What can a few brave men do against so many thousands ?

Quid paucus fortis facio contra tot mille ?

13. Say, ye Muses, what is the origin of the sacred-rites.

Dico Pĭĕrĭs (-ĭdis) quis origo sacer (*neut. pl.*) sum.

14. The ancients are said to have worshipped Pan, the god of cattle.

Vetus fero colo Pan (*acc.* Pānă) deus pecus.

15. No bull used to pant beneath the curved ploughshare.

Nullus taurus anhelo sub aduncus vomer.

16. And while the attendants prepare the banquet and wine to be drunk.

Dumque minister paro epulae vinum (*pl.*) que pōto.

17. There was more praise in the sword than in the curved plough.

Plus laus '(*gen.*) sum in gladius quam curvus aratrum.

18. He lying on-his-face gave kisses to mother earth.

Ille jaceo pronus osculum mater terra do.

19. Meanwhile Ardea is encompassed with Roman standards.

Interea Ardea cingo Romanus signum.

20. She ends in tears and lets-go the threads begun.

Desino in lacrima remitto que fila incipio.

21. Now the bird, harbinger of daylight, had uttered its strains.

Jam ales praenuntius lux do cantus.

EXERCISE XII.

IN this Exercise the cæsura is the hephthemimeral; the lines beginning as before with a dactyl, and there being no elisions.

1. When Aurora had moved away the cold shades from the sky.

   Cum Aurora dimoveo gelidus umbra polus.

2. Anna replies: O more beloved to thy sister than the light.

   Anna refero: o magis dilectus soror lux (*case after comp. ?*)

3. While stormy-weather and rainy Orion spend-their-rage on the deep.

   Dum hiems et aquosus Ŏrīon desaevio (*sing.*) pelagus.

4. She displays the treasures of-Sidon and the city prepared.

   Ostento Sidonius opes urbs que paro.

5. The charger stands and champs, high-spirited, his foaming bit.

   Sonipes sto ac mando ferox spumans frenum (*pl.*)

6. In alarm they sought shelter; streams flow-down from the mountains.

   Metus peto tectum (*pl.*); amnis ruo de mons.

7. Rouse ye, my men, in haste, and take your seats on the thwarts.

   Vigilo, vir, praeceps (*nom. pl.*) et consido transtrum.

8. They quit the shore; the sea is hidden beneath the fleets.

   Desero (*pf. in* -ere) litus (*pl*); aequor lateo sub classis.

D

9. When the ships gained the open-sea, the south-winds
   blowing.

   Ut ratis teneo pelagus, auster spiro (*abl. abs*)

10. Father Aeneas stood-aghast, and thus he speaks.

    Pater Aeneas obstupesco ac talis (*neut. pl.*) for.

11. Nor did his cheeks lack tears while the sailor lingers.

    Nec gena careo lacrima (*abl.*) dum nauta moror.

12. He stood before the feet of Euryalus and demands the prize.

    Sto ante pes Euryălus et posco praemium (*pl.*)

13. And he bids a shield to be brought forth, the work of
    Didymaon.

    Et clipeus jubeo efferro, ars (*acc. pl.*) Didymāōn (-ŏnĭs).

14. Where he had sat down next-him on a green mound
    of turf.

    Ut consideo proximus viridans torus herba.

15. The youth of Sicily and of Troy murmur in-admiration.

    Juventus Trinacria Trojaque fremo miror (*pf. ptcp.*)

16. I come hither by Jove's command, a wanderer and an
    exile.

    Huc venio imperium Jupiter, peregrinus et exsul.

17. Lightly he speeds in his azure car over the surface of
    the waves.

    Levis volo caeruleus axis super summus aequor (*pl.*)

18. He, accompanying my journey through a thousand
    dangers.

    Ille, comitor (*pf. ptcp.*) meus iter per periclum mille.

19. Have pity on an infirm old man, to whom few things
    remain.

    Misereor invalidus senex (*case ?*) qui paucus supersum.

20. Dutiful Aeneas performs the commands of the Sibyl.

    Pius Aeneas exsequor praeceptum Sibylla.

EXERCISE XIII.

In the following lines examples of both cæsuras will be found, and the first foot will not necessarily be a dactyl. There are still no elisions.

1. The Argive chieftains have returned, the altars are smoking.

   Dux Argolicus redeo, altare fumo.
2. Brides bring grateful offerings for husbands safe.

   Nympha fero gratum donum pro maritus salvus.
3. Whoever steers a foreign bark towards these shores.

   Quisquis verto peregrinus navis ad hic litus.
4. He is moved, however, by my dutifulness and prayers.

   Ille moveo tamen meus pietas precesque.
5. Nor have I strength to drive foes from dwelling.

   Nec vis (*pl.*) sum ego (*case ?*) inimicus tectum pello.
6. Four times the moon was hidden; four times it grew again with full orb.

   Quater luna lateo ; quater recresco plenus orbis.
7. And to mingle my tears with thy tears.

   Confundo que noster lacrima cum tuus lacrima.
8. Why pray I, unhappy one ? another spouse now holds thee.

   Quid infelix precor ? alter conjux (*fem.*) jam tu teneo.
9. Whether the ground is thawed in the day-time, or continues cold.

   Sive humus laxo dies, seu duro frigidus.

10. A captive woman, I shall follow a conqueror, sad to be said.

Captiva sequor victor, miserabilis dico (*supine*).

11. Nor think it base for thee to yield to my prayers.

Nec puto turpis tu succumbo preces noster.

12. 'Tis safer to have lain on couch, than to grasp weapons.

Tutus sum jaceo torus, quam teneo telum.

13. Thou dost hurl the pliant shaft with sturdy arm.

Tu torqueo lentus hastile validus lacertus.

14. Who showed thee the glens fit for hunting ?

Quis monstro tu saltus venatus (*pl.*) aptus ?

15. The beech-trees carved by thee bear my name.

Fagus incido a tu servo meum nomen (*pl.*)

16. But when thou wast poor and didst drive herds (as) a shepherd.

At cum sum pauper, pastor que ago armentum.

17. I indeed was not at-ease, and was ever afraid.

Non sum equidem securus (*fem.*), semperque vereor.

18. Thou hadst gone from hence my husband ; thou returnedst thence not my husband.

Eo hinc meus vir ; redeo inde non meus vir.

19. With what countenance wouldst thou look on thy children, guilty one, with what (countenance wouldst thou look on) me ?

Qui vultus video natus, qui ego, sceleratus ?

20. Would that thou too wert changeable equally-with the winds.

Utinam tu quoque sum mutabilis cum ventis.

EXERCISE XIV.

ON THE PENTAMETER.

THE formation of this line has been described above
(p. 7). The strictness of the limits within which it is
confined allows less variety than can be attained in the
hexameter. While more monotonous, it is thus easier of
imitation for the learner. The main rules to be observed
are :—

(1.) That while in the first half of the line two dactyls, or
two spondees, or one of each, may stand, followed by
a long syllable ; in the second half two dactyls alone
may be used, followed by a syllable either long or
short. The commonest type is that in which a
dactyl begins, followed by a spondee, as—

Quo tamen adversis fluctibus ire paras ?

(2.) While a long syllable is spoken of as ending each half
of the line, as in the scheme

$$ \left. \begin{array}{c} -\ - \\ -\ \smile\ \smile \end{array} \right| \left. \begin{array}{c} -\ - \\ -\ \smile\ \smile \end{array} \right| \left. \begin{array}{c} - \end{array} \right| -\ \smile\ \smile \left. \right| -\ \smile\ \smile \left. \right| \overset{\smile}{-} $$

the learner must not suppose that a *monosyllable* is
meant by it. In point of fact, a monosyllable can
only stand at the end of the line when there is an
elision before *est*, as in

Grande morae pretium tuta futura via est,

and at the end of the first half when there is either
such an elision, as in

Irrita, qua visum est, ventus et unda ferunt,

or another monosyllable preceding, as in

> Artifices in te verte, Minerva, manus,

or a dissyllable ($\smile \smile$) equal in time to one long syllable, as in

> Inque vicem tua me, te mea forma capit.

It is obvious that there is in this instance a special
effect of antithesis to be gained ; and the learner will
do well to avoid all monosyllabic endings at first.

(3.) The word ending the pentameter must be a dissyllable, and must also be either a substantive, verb, or
personal or possessive pronoun.   In the early stages
of practice this rule also should be made absolute.
By and by it may be seen that a word of four syllables, or preferably one of five, has a beauty of its
own, if used with discrimination, as in

> Nec sedeo duris torva superciliis,
>
> Unda simul miserum vitaque deseruit ;

or that an adverb may be placed at the end with
fine effect, as in the well-known line of Tibullus
(iii. 6. 56)—

> Perfida, sed, quamvis perfida, cara tamen.

But these touches of the master's art are not for the
beginner to imitate.   A word of three syllables must
on no account end the line.

(4.) A word ending in a consonant, or in a long vowel, is
best for the close of a pentameter.   Of the short
vowels, final $\breve{e}$ is commoner than final $\breve{a}$.

(5.) While a similarity of ending, or even rhyme, is often
met with in the two halves of the pentameter, a line

constructed of two exactly similar halves is inelegant.
For instance—

> Spes tua lenta fuit : quod petis, alter habet

is only tolerable as a rare variety; while such a
type as—

> Protinus illa meos auguror esse deos

should be altogether avoided.   And, in general, the
line will be most pleasing to the ear when the first
half is of such construction that it could not be made
to stand as the second half, as—

> Non quia tu dignus, sed quia mitis ego.
> Denaque luciferos luna movebat equos.

EXERCISE XV.

WRITE each of the following as the second half of a pentameter :—

1. Glory was sweet   gloria sum dulcia.
2. Has love fled so quickly ?   amor fugio tam cito ?
3. Mars favouring the heroes   Mars (*abl. abs.*) faveo vir.
4. A boar to be feared with   aper timeo dens.
   tusk
5. Left a prey to wild-beasts   relinquo (*fem. pass. ptcp.*)
                                  praeda fera.
6. He was safe from the enemy   sum tutus ab hostis.
7. The father himself gives a   pater ipse do via.
   way
8. The palace echoes with   regia sono vox.
   voice

9. That he might bring thee help ... ut fero opem tu.

10. With ploughshare thou cleavest the ground ... findo humus vomer.

11. To be a messenger of woe ... sum nuntius malum.

12. None shall be unavenged ... nullus sum inultus.

13. Our eyes are wet (with tears) ... lumen noster madeo.

14. There was nought save sea ... nil sum nisi pontus.

15. To say the sad (word) Farewell ... dico tristis " Vale."

16. She falls overcome by fear ... cado vinco timor.

17. Nor will the enemy be far-off ... nec hostis sum procul.

18. Have a care for me ... sum tu cura ego (gen.)

19. His right hand refuses its task ... dextra opus recuso.

20. The handle slipped from his hand ... ansa excido manus.

21. The rich man abounds in horses ... dives equus abundo.

22. He will be like a soldier ... sum instar miles (gen.)

23. Great prizes stimulate ... magnus praemium moveo.

24. Wert thou a guest or an enemy ? ... sum hospes an hostis ?

EXERCISE XVI.

WRITE each of the following as the first half of a pentameter.   The sense will often be incomplete.

1. Though I should try	quamvis experior.
2. The gods are witnesses to me	di sum testis ego.
3. He discharges his duty	officium fungor.
4. Liberty has been given	libertas do.
5. To manners and to life	mos et vita.
6. And though thou hast no hope	cumque spero nihil.
7. Turn thy countenance, I pray	flecto vultus, precor.
8. And where he made a way	quaque facio via.
9. In winds and water	in ventus et aqua.
10. Having promised sureties	polliceor pignus.
11. Give pardon to a wearied one	venia do fassus.
12. A stronger intellect	fortis ingenium.
13. And to prevent thee from coming	quoque minus venio.
14. What I am to follow is in doubt	in dubius sum quis sequor.
15. He returned with booty	redeo cum praeda.
16. Not I by nature	non natura ego.
17. Lo ! I write again	en ! scribo iterum.
18. A thousand stratagems remain	dolus mille resto.
19. He who serves so well	qui servio tam bene.
20. In time of marrying	nubo tempus.
21. Nor can I say	nec possum dico.
22. Whom I should least wish	qui volo minime.
23. You ought to have yielded	debeo (*plup.*) cedo.
24. And save thyself as well	simul que servo tu.

EXERCISE XVII.

THE following are for entire pentameters :—

1. Such were the words of oracular Jove.
   Talis sum (*pf.* fuere) dictum fatidicus Jupiter.
2. Each bank was pasturing cattle scattered-about.
   Uterque ripa pasco bos spargo.
3. The half will be greater than the whole gift.
   Dimidium major sum totus munus.
4. Then the goddess herself removed the fears she caused.
   Tum dea ipse tollo metus qui facio.
5. Why did they entrust a golden sceptre to my hand ?
   Cur do aureus sceptrum (*pl.*) meus dextra ?
6. Stay ye your tears ; I myself, she says, will heal.
   Sisto tu lacrima ; ipse, ait, medeor.
7. This title did prolonged old age give him.
   Hic titulus longus senecta do ille.
8. There is there a little column of no little mark.
   Sum ibi parvus columna non parvus nŏta (*gen.*)
9. And they placed him on the Quirinal hill.
   Consisto que in Quĭrīnalis jugum.
10. My daughter, in whose safety (= who being safe) I shall
    ever be happy.
    Filia, qui sospes semper sum felix.
11. That day, on which vows are paid to the goddess.
    Ille dies (*fem. when* = set day) qui votum solutus sum
    dea.
12. If it is allowed us to come to thy sacred-rites.
    Si licet ego ad tuus sacrum venio.

EXERCISE XVIII.

(*The same continued.*)

1. Many gifts I gave, many I was about to give.
   Multus munus do, multus sum daturus.
2. And the broad shores that lie open to my eyes.
   Latus que litus qui pateo meus oculus (*begin with relat.*)
3. Thou wilt be known either by this or by a like strain.
   Notus sum aut hic aut similis carmen.
4. Thou wert to me a lord, thou a husband, thou a brother.
   Tu sum ego dominus, tu vir, tu frater.
5. I am not a great load for thy fleet.
   Ego non sum magna sarcina tua classis.
6. And Greece lies sorrowful before thy feet.
   Et Graecia jaceo maestus ante tuus pes.
7. Constrain (her) to die, whom thou constrainest to live without thee.
   Cogo morior, qui cogo vivo sine tu (*begin with relat.*)
8. And the horse taken from the herd scarce endures reins.
   Equus que capio de grex vix patior frenum.
9. The blue wave receives the ships when-launched.
   Caerulus unda accipio ratis deductus.
10. And may the bones of old Anchises lie softly.
    Et os senex Anchises cubo molliter.
11. At which time true dreams are wont to be seen.
    Qui tempus verus somnium soleo cerno.
12. And the moist earth is-green with unfading turf.
    Udusque terra vireo perpetuus gramen.

EXERCISE XIX.

ON THE COUPLET.

AFTER mastering the hexameter and pentameter separately the learner will still find some guidance necessary in forming that combination of the two which is called a distich, or couplet. This is chiefly because the division of sentences has now to be considered, as well as the metrical limits of the lines. A sentence may be completed and another begun in either line, or one continuous sentence may occupy the two. With very rare exceptions, the sense of every couplet should be complete in itself, and not carried on from a pentameter to a fresh hexameter. The flowing run, which is a chief beauty in Virgilian hexameters, is not compatible with the terse neatness and compact finish of the elegiac metre. Even the first line of the couplet should more often than not be complete in itself. When the sense runs on, the pentameter will best begin with a dactyl, and the end of this dactyl is a good place for making the end of the clause, as in

> Ilion adspicies firmataque turribus altis
> Moenia, Phoebeae structa canore lyrae.

Another good place for the pause to come, though much less common than the above, is after the second syllable of the opening dactyl, as in

> Ter tecum conata loqui, ter inutilis haesit
> Lingua, ter in primo destitit ore sonus.

The sense may also, of course, be carried on to the mid
division of the line, or uninterruptedly to the end.   Less
usual breaks are those after the third half-foot, as in

> Pliada, si quaeres, in nostra gente Jovemque
> Invenies, medios ut taceamus avos,

and still less usual those a syllable later, as—

> Vidi consortes pariter generisque necisque
> Tres cecidisse : tribus, quae mihi, mater erat.

To give a tone of weight or impressiveness, the pause may
come after an opening spondee, as in

> Nulla Mycenaeum sociasse cubilia mecum
> Juro : fallentem deseruisse velis.

A pause at the end of a third long syllable, when the sense
is carried on from the hexameter, is said to have no example
in Ovid.

As a general rule, it may be laid down that, where no
special effect is intended, it is better to begin the pentameter with a dactyl than with a spondee ; and, if both the
first feet are spondees, then the longer word should precede the shorter.   Thus—

> Pugnabit caute respicietque domum

is written by Ovid in preference to

> Caute pugnabit respicietque domum.

But the desire of having two words in agreement at the
end of the two halves of the line, or considerations of
sound, of antithesis, and the like, make this rule subject
to many exceptions.   It is thus easy to see why Ovid
wrote

> Et cogor lacrimas combibere ipsa meas,

instead of

> Et lacrimas cogor, etc.,

or again,

> Dicar privigno fida noverca meo,

instead of beginning with the longer word.   These niceties
may not require much attention from the learner at first ;
but it is as well for him to acquire betimes a perception of
what the ancient masters of versification regarded as harmonious.

EXERCISE XX.

RENDER into elegiac couplets—

1. There is, near the purple hills of flowery Hymettus,
     A sacred fount, and ground soft with green turf.

   Sum, prope purpureus collis florens Hymettus,
     Sacer fons, et humus mollis viridis caespes.

2. And now mid day had shortened the scanty shadows,
     And evening and morning were at an equal dis-
       tance.

   Jamque medius dies contraho tenuis umbra,
     Vesper que et ortus sum in par spatium.

3. Keep-following me on the pinions given (thee) ; I will
     go in-advance ;
       Be it thy care to follow ; under my guidance thou
         wilt be safe.

   Sector ego pinna datus ; ego eo praevius ;
     Tuus cura sum sequor : ego dux (abl.) sum tutus.

4. And now on-the-point-of-flying he kissed his little
    son,
      Nor did the father's cheeks repress tears.

   Jamque volo (*fut. ptcp.*) do osculum parvus natus,
     Nec patrius (*adj.*) gena contineo lacrima.

5. The slaves were weeping apart, and hiding their
    tears :
      Who would wish to be the messenger of so great
      a sorrow ?

   Servus fleo diversus tego que lacrima :
     Quis volo sum nuntius tantus malum ?

6. And yet he would have kept the duty of hospitality
    to the last,
      But he feared the great power of Pygmalion.

   Et tamen servo munus hospitium ad ultimus (*neut. pl.*)
     Sed magnus opes Pygmălĭōn timeo.

EXERCISE XXI.

(*The same continued.*)

1. While she sits, the shady osiers and tuneful birds
    Brought slumber, and the light rippling of the water.

   Dum sedeo, umbrosus salix canorus que volucris
     Facio somnus (*pl.*) et levis murmur aqua.

2. Gentle repose stole unperceived over her vanquished
    eyes,
  And her arm, become drooping, sank from her chin.

  Blandus quies obrepo furtim vinco ocellus,
    Et manus factus languidus cado mentum.

3. Thence, marvellous to behold, two palm-trees together
    Rise : one of them was taller (than the other).

  Iude, mirabilis video (*abl. of sup.*), duo palma pariter
    Surgo : alter ex ille sum magnus.

4. The citizens overjoyed at the omen lay the foundations,
    And in a little time there was a new wall.

  Civis laetus augurium jacio fundamen,
    Et exiguus tempus sum novus murus.

5. Thrice essaying flight, she thrice paused by the deep
    waters,
  Fear taking-away the power of running.

  Ter molior fuga, ter resisto ad altus unda,
    Metus eripio (*abl. abs.*) vis (*pl.*) curro.

6. Now the hosts were standing, prepared for the sword
    and for death,
    Now the clarion was about-to-give the signal for
    the fight.

  Jam acies sto (*plup.*) paratus ferrum morsque,
    Jam lituus sum daturus signum (*pl.*) pugna.

EXERCISE XXII.

THE learner may now prepare to enter on the more inter-
esting stage of verse-making, that of translating into
Latin short passages from the English poets. For some
time he can only attempt this by the help of a retranslation; and it is here that the great difficulty and the great
test of his powers will arise. Many young scholars attain
with ease the ability to render into Elegiacs lines set in a
form for retranslation. But when they are confronted
with a passage in its original state, their ability seems to
fail them. They cannot throw the expressions of the
English poet into a form that adapts itself to the Latin
metre.

It is of such great importance to acquire a power of
doing this, and the failures of beginners at this critical
stage are so many, that it is worth while, even thus early,
to spend a little time in analysing a number of actual
renderings, the work of different scholars, and learning,
if possible, something of the secret of their art. We will
begin with very simple instances; and the student must
imagine himself at work upon them, trying to translate
them for himself.

Speaking of flowers, Byron says—

> Such in her chaplet infant Dian wove,
> And Innocence would offer to her love.

As we try to think of the chief words, those which cannot
well be neglected, or materially changed, it will occur that

E

corona or *corolla* is the natural word for " chaplet," and will stand readily at the end of the hexameter. " Dian," or *Diana*, is marked out by its quantity to precede it. Thus we have the end provided for, which is always the most important part to think of first. As the first of *Diana* may be long, what should prevent *infans* from standing before it ? In like manner " such" (flowers) can most simply be *tales*, and as *plico* is the regular word for " weave," *implico* will be " to weave in ;" and so the line seems to fashion itself into

Implicuit tales infans Diana corollae, *or* corollis.

If all were as easy as this, the art would be soon acquired. But we must not be too sanguine. What is to become of the pentameter ? Is " Innocence " to be *innocentia*, and " to her love" *amori suo* ? If so, then neither of the cardinal words can be brought in. Now comes a caution that will be often needed. In English we are fond of abstract terms; in Latin the ancient writers were not. We talk of " Innocence offering " ; they would personify, and talk of " an innocent person offering." They even carried the principle so far as to prefer, in poetry at least, names of special winds, seas, and the like, to general appellations of the elements. We talk of " casting care to the winds." Horace says : " Tradam protervis in mare *Creticum* portare ventis." Why should " care " be cast into the " Cretan Sea " more than into any other ? The reason is to be found in the principle stated above. It is akin to the instinct that made Sir Walter Scott, when describing the flashing of a beacon light, name the mountain peaks it passed along, instead of using the simple term mountain-heights.

Applying now this principle to the line before us, for "Innocence" we shall think of *innocens puella*, or something similar, and for "love," *puer*, or something like it; though *amor* may in fact be used of persons. With these hints, *puella suo* comes naturally at the end of the line, and *puero* at the end of the first half. Then what is to replace the unmanageable *innocens?* Plainly some feminine adjective, of kindred meaning, to stand before *puella*. Rejecting *pura*, because of the alliteration, it would not be hard to think of *casta*. "And would offer" being literally *et offerat*, or *offerat et*, the result is

Offerat et puero casta puella suo.

For the next instance, a couplet of Longfellow's may be chosen, as containing words that will now be familiar :—

He bound his brow with a woodbine wreath,
And smil'd his playful eye.

Here a difficulty of an elementary kind arises and one that will recur at every turn for some time. How are the Latin words to be found for unusual terms, such as "woodbine"? Is an English-Latin dictionary to be resorted to? Of course it must, in many cases, but the learner should try at the outset to use his own resources first as much as possible. If he cannot recall the exact Latin word for an English one, let him think of an English synonym for the latter; this will often suggest a fair equivalent. But "woodbine" or "honeysuckle" may be reasonably expected to puzzle him. The dictionary will probably give *periclymenus*, not a very convenient word, and wanting in poetical authority, except as a proper name. Here, then, as often, the question will arise, whether "woodbine" is of such

consequence to the thought that it must be translated, or
whether some more general epithet for "wreath" will do
instead.   If the latter is determined upon, it will be easy
(after the experience of the previous couplet, and noting
also that the reference is to a boy at play) to write :

> Implicuit virides fronti puer ille corollas.

The pentameter, we soon see, will have to be considerably
altered in form.   If we set down the simple equivalents for
the words, *et risit jocosus oculus*, it is plain that nothing can
be done with them.   Here, it must be confessed, is a kind
of stumbling-block that nothing can carry the learner very
easily over.   A few hints may smooth the way.   As he
tries to grasp the thought, as much as he can, independently
of particular words, he will find that it could be expressed
just as well by "there was a smile on his playful countenance," or "there was a playful smile on his face," or something of that kind.   At this point *risus in ore* may start
into his mind ; and, if so, the difficulty is over.   *Risus in ore
fuit* is the latter half, and all that remains is the choice of
appropriate epithets for the nouns, such as—

> Liber et innocuo risus in ore fuit.

The next example will serve to introduce a method,
necessary at times, of *transposing* the order of the English
lines, so as to be more suitable to the requirements of the
metre.   Such a liberty must not, of course, be taken with
the original unless there is some real advantage to be
gained.   The couplet is from Warton—

> To the deep wood the clamorous rooks repair ;
>   Light skims the swallow o'er the wat'ry scene.

As we think of the two essential words, "rook" and "swallow," in Latin *cornix* and *hirundo*, it is obvious that the latter is much more available for the hexameter than for the pentameter. Nor is there anything in the sense to forbid the transposition of the lines. We shall thus be tempted to start with the idea of placing *hirundo* at the end of the hexameter. "Light" will of course be *leviter*, or *levis*, qualifying the verb like an adverb, as an adjective often does in Latin; but for "skims" and "watery scene" we shall have to pause and reflect. Does "skims" imply flight through the air or scudding over the surface of the water? Will *transvolo, transvolito,* or *trano,* be the word? Again, how is "scene" to be expressed? The Romans had no general term for "scene," or "landscape," any more than for "picturesque." Their way was to localize and personify, to talk of "Thessala Tempe," and the like. But as we think of swallows scudding over water, the surface of a lake or pond at once presents itself to the imagination. This may suggest *stagna* as a suitable word to begin with. It may now occur to us to combine the two ideas of scudding over the lake and flitting through the air, as there is not a press of words for the verse. One verb will then be a participle governing *stagna*, or else *aera* or *aethera*, and the other will govern the remaining noun. And as *tranat* comes conveniently before *hirundo,* we shall soon see our way to—

Stagna supervolitans levis aethera tranat hirundo.

In the pentameter we shall have to resort to an expedient that is of very frequent application. That is, placing a noun-clause in apposition, instead of an epithet. The

example will make this clear. "Rooks," we said, was
córnícēs, and "repair to the wood" will naturally be *petunt
silvam.* Hence it will seem desirable to begin and end with
cornices . . . petunt. But now what is to be done with
"clamorous"? *Raucus* would be a suitable word, but if
we write *cornices raucae,* what is to become of "deep wood"?
Here comes the benefit of the resource just mentioned.
Just as the "mounted peasantry" would be conveniently
turned by "equites, rustica turba," or "crowded retinue"
by "comites, magna caterva," so "clamorous rooks" may
be neatly expressed by "cornices, garrula turba." Hence
we obtain—

> Cornices silvas, garrula turba, petunt.

One more instance must suffice. Suppose the task be
to translate Tennyson's

> Lady Clara Vere de Vere,
> Of me you shall not win renown.

It is assumed that in this, as in the other couplets chosen,
the learner has enough of the context before him to enable
him to see what the drift of the passage is. Here it is a
proud lady of high family who is addressed. It will
accordingly be a first point for consideration, how to find
some equivalent for the proper name which may accord
with this. *Clara* is, of course, Latin, but it was not used
as a proper name. And though there was an emperor
Verus, it would be a poor conceit to invent some phrase
expressing, "sprung from Verus." One whose reading
might recall to him Horace's

> Aeli, vetusto nobilis ab Lamo,

or Juvenal's

> Stemmata quid faciunt? quid prodest, Pontice, longo
> Sanguine censeri, etc.,

would have the materials at hand for rendering Tennyson's
line with effect. And this may suggest the advantage, or
rather the necessity, of storing up in the memory as many
lines and sentences from the Roman poets as can be done.
But one who is learning from this book is not likely to
have read Horace or Juvenal. We must see, then, what
can be done without that. "Haughty maiden, of high
birth,"—that is the central thought. Such phrases as
virgo nobilis, celso de sanguine, antiqua de stirpe, superba puella,
and the like, could not be far to seek. One who could not
recall any special names of proud Roman families, such as
the Appii, might still know that the Romans associated the
idea of haughtiness with their ancient kings. Hence he
might produce—

> Nobilis antiqua veniens de stirpe puella,

or—

> Nobilis antiquo regum de sanguine virgo.

For the pentameter he will find, as often, that a literal
translation, such as *non de me laudem paries,* though metrical in form, will not answer. He must think of the
ending; and for this purpose nominative cases, as a rule,
are more serviceable than accusatives. Try the sentence
passively: "renown shall not be won by you from me."
This would naturally suggest *non parietur honor* as the ending. That is something; but it may be felt that *honor* is
not quite the word. The idea is rather that of triumph.
The speaker will not let himself be led captive. Hence

triumphus may do better—*triumphus erit* sounds promising.
Non or *nullus* will most likely begin. Still something is
wanting, especially something to stand before *triumphus*.
What is to replace *me* in *non tibi de . . . me . . . triumphus
erit ?* As it is an affair of the affections, *de amore meo, de
nostro pectore*, etc., may be tried, until *de nostro corde* is
thought of, and there ensues—

> Non tibi de nostro corde triumphus erit.

The learner may observe in passing that *nos* and *noster*
may be freely used for *ego* and *meus*, but not *vos* and *vester*
for *tu* and *tuus*.

EXERCISE XXIII.

IN this and the following Exercises, as space will not
admit of any such analysis as that given above, the learner
should carefully compare the original English with the
retranslation, couplet by couplet, and endeavour to see
why the change of form in each case has been made.
For the order in which the Latin words are given, see the
note to Exercise V.

1. By day along the astonish'd land
       The cloudy pillar glided slow.

> At early morn, the people wondering far and wide, the
>   column
>   Was like a cloud, and was drawing itself on the
>   ground.

> Mane novus, populus (*abl. abs.*) miror late, columna
> Sum instar nubes, traho que se humi.

2. By night Arabia's crimson'd sands
   Return'd the fiery column's glow.

   At night it traversed the reddening sands of the Arabs:
   The whole ground shone-again with the reflected
   light.

   Nox lustro rubesco arena Arabs:
   Totus humus reluceo repercussus lux.

3. Like the leaves of the forest, when summer is green,
   That host with their banners at sunset were seen.

   Like forest leaves, when summer has burst-into-flower,
   The hour of eventide sees the bands with standards.

   Veluti silvestris frons, cum aestas floresco,
   Hora vesper video agmen cum signum.

4. Like the leaves of the forest, when autumn hath blown,
   That host on the morrow lay withered and strown.

   Like forest leaves, after the colds of winter,
   The morrow's light saw (them) everywhere strewn on
   the ground.

   Veluti silvestris frons, post frigus bruma,
   Crastinus lux video (*imp.*) passim stratus (*n. pl.*) humi.

5. Nay, smile not at my sullen brow;
   Alas! I cannot smile again.

   Forbear to laugh-at the cloud of a stern brow:
   Alas! I am unable myself to return thy laughter.

   Mitto rideo nubes severus supercilium;
   Heu nequeo ipse refero tuus risus (*pl.*)

6. When Gondoline roam'd along the shore,
    A maiden full fair to the sight.

    Hither (and) thither with rapid step Laodamia roams,
        Wandering through a sweet spot, herself sweeter.

    Huc illuc rapidus pes Lăŏdămīa vagor,
        Devius per suavis locus ipse suavis.

EXERCISE XXIV.

(*The same continued.*)

1. But when the sun in all his state
    Illumed the eastern skies.

    But when the sun in-its-splendour had dispelled the
        uncertain shades,
        When the golden light is ruddy in the whole east.

    At cum sol splendeo (*part.*) discutio dubius umbra,
        Cum aureus lux rubeo totus oriens.

2. Be hush'd, be hush'd, ye bitter winds,
    Ye pelting rains, a little rest.

    But do ye, O blasts of the cold wind, be hushed,
        Nor let the shower of rain always fall.

    At vos, o flamen gelidus ventus, taceo (*pres. subj.*),
        Nec imber pluvius aqua semper decido.

3. These (flowers) owe their birth to genial May ;
    Beneath a fiercer sun they pine.

The more genial breeze of May fosters those flowers ;
  Roses droop beneath a hotter sky.

Genialis aura Maius foveo ille flos ;
  Rosa langueo sub fervidus caelum.

4. The summer is short, and the winter must come,
    With her hail and her storm and her snows.

  Alas ! summer is short, times of winter will soon come,
    And dreadful snow-storms, and icy frost.

  Heu ! aestas sum brevis, tempus bruma cito venio,
    Horrendusque nix et glacialis gelu.

5. 'Tis night, and the landscape is lovely no more :
    I mourn, but, ye woodlands, I mourn not for you.

  Night falls, and the beauty of forest and of country
      sinks in shade :
      Not for thee, country, not for thee, forest, will I
        utter sighs.

  Nox ruo, et decus silva et rus occido umbra :
    Non tu, rus, non tu, silva, do gemitus.

6. I loved thee once, I'll love no more ;
    Thine be the grief, as is the blame.

  Once a faithful lover, henceforth I disdain love ;
    To thee, who hast deserved blame, be grief by right.

  Olim fidus amans, posthac aspernor amor ;
    Qui (*fem.*) meritus sum culpa, sum tu dolor jus.

PART II.

* *The Latin words required for Exercises XXV.-L. will be found in the Vocabulary at the end.*

EXERCISE XXV.

YOUNG Paris was the shepherds' pride,
    As well the fair Oenone knew ;
They sat the mountain stream beside,
    And o'er the bank a poplar grew.

Upon the bark this verse he traced—
    " Bear witness to the vow I make :
Thou, Xanthus, to thy source shalt haste,
    Ere I my matchless maid forsake."

Back to thy source now, Xanthus, run ;
    Paris is now a prince of Troy :
He leaves the fair his flattery won,
    Himself and country to destroy.

RETRANSLATION.

That Paris was the shepherds' pride, than whom no other
    (was) more beautiful,
  Oenōnē knew, alas! a trustful nymph.
They used to recline together on the margin of a moun-
    tain stream,
  Where a white poplar quivers with its leaves on the
    bank.
This verse the youth engraved on the rugged bark,   5
  And dared to call the gods to (hear) his vows :

"When there is (one) like to thee, when I endure to live
    without thee,
  The water of Xanthus shall turn and run back to its
    source."

Xanthus, hasten backward, and ye waves turn and run back,
  That youth is recognised of Trojan blood.   10

Forsworn he leaves the loving (maiden) won by his
    flatteries,
  That he may ruin both himself and his own country.

Hints.

1. "Paris," in the accusative, *Parin*. This word will end line 2. "Pride," *decus*.

8. "Turn and run back," *versa recurret*. Observe that a participle and verb will often best translate two verbs in English joined by a conjunction. This line and the next are from Ovid, *Her.* v. 28, 29.

10. "Of," sign of ablative. "Trojan," *Dardănius*.

12. "His own," *ipse suam*. The possessive pronouns "his," "her," etc., are generally to be left untranslated, unless when emphatic, as here. When that is the case, *ipse* is often added.

EXERCISE XXVI.

On the holy mount of Ida,
  Where the pine and cypress grow,
Sate a young and lovely woman,
  Weeping ever, weeping low:
Drearily throughout the forest
  Did the winds of autumn blow,
And the clouds above were flying,
  And Scamander rolled below.

"Faithless Paris! cruel Paris!"
  Thus the poor deserted spake—
"Wherefore thus so strangely leave me?
  Why thy loving bride forsake?
Why no tender word at parting,
  Why no kiss, no farewell take?
Would that I could but forget thee!
  Would this throbbing heart might break!"
                   AYTOUN.

RETRANSLATION.

There is a spot in the woodland valleys of holy Ida;
  Pine-trees stand around, nor is the cypress wanting:
Alone on the ground was sitting a lovely woman; you
    might see
  That her cheeks were wet with constant weeping;
You might hear amid the recesses of the thick forest   5
  The force of the autumn wind resounding mournfully.
Above, the clouds were hurrying-along in the overcast sky;
  Before her feet, Xanthus was moving-on its swelling
    waters.
Cruel Paris, and the perjuries of a false tongue
  She tells of, left alone by a faithless man.   10
"A credulous spouse, I am abandoned by my spouse," she
    cries;
  "Paris has the heart to have forsaken Oenone.
Why didst thou give me no kisses at parting? at least
  Thy treacherous tongue ought to have said Farewell!
May the fates grant (me) to forget both thy guile and thee. 15
  In a word, for what remains, may the fates grant me
    to die!"

F

HINTS.

1. " Woodland," *nemorosus.*

2. " Cypress." Besides *cŭpressus,* a form *cyparissus* is found Virg. *Aen.* iii. 680.

4. " Were wet," perf. inf. of *immadesco.* Comp Ov *Tr.* i. 9. ?

6. Lit. " the autumnal force of the south-wind "   " Mournfull; *triste.*

7. " Overcast," *obscuro.*

12. Ov. *Her.* v. 30.

15. " Both thy guile and thee :" end with *dolique tuique.*

16. " For what remains," *quod restat.*

EXERCISE XXVII.

EVEN so the gentle Tyrian dame,
  When neither grief nor love prevail,
Saw the dear object of her flame,
  Th' ungrateful Trojan, hoist his sail.
Aloud she call'd on him to stay ;
The wind bore him and her lost words away.

The doleful Ariadne so
  On the wide shore forsaken stood :
" False Theseus, whither dost thou go ?"
  Afar false Theseus cut the flood.
But Bacchus came to her relief :—
Bacchus himself's too weak to ease my grief.
                                        COWLEY.

RETRANSLATION.

As once the Phœnician queen, of a suppliant
  When neither the voice nor love had availed enough,

Looking-forth from the walls, saw the beloved Æneas,

   Forgetful of his pledge, loosening the cables of his bark ;

In vain, invoking the gods, she tried-to-recall the hero

     when-on-his-way ;   5

   The same winds had carried-away vows and bark.

Even so the Gnossian maid was bewailing her hard lot,

   Left alone on the shore of a deserted sea :

" Whither fliest thou ?" she cries, "guilty Theseus, return!"

   But he was cleaving far away the waters of-the-deep. 10

Bacchus by his coming brought safety to thee, Cretan

    maid,

   But even Bacchus himself is unequal to my woes.

HINTS.

1. " As," *ac* . . . *velut.*   " Of a suppliant," *precantis.*

2. " Enough," *tantum.*

4. " Loosening " (inf)

5 "Tried to recall," imperf. tense.   " When on his way,"
euntem.

6. " The same," *idem* (pl.) Comp. Ov *Her.* vii. 8.

7 "Gnossian maid," *Gnosis,* feminine appellative from Gnosus,
or Gnossus, a town in Crete.   So *Cressa* for "Cretan maid," in line 11.

9 This line is from Ovid, *Her.* x. 35.

11. "Bacchus," *Liber.*   "By his coming," *adveniens.*

12. "Unequal to," *minor,* with abl.

EXERCISE XXVIII.

A PICTURE.

HERE let the wretched Ariadne stand,

Seduced by Theseus to some desart land ;

Her locks dishevel'd waving in the wind;
The crystal tears confess her tortur'd mind.
The perjur'd youth unfurls his treach'rous sails,
And their white bosoms catch the swelling gales.
Be still! ye winds, she cries; stay Theseus, stay!
But faithless Theseus hears no more than they.
All desperate, to some craggy cliff she flies,
And spreads a well-known signal in the skies.
His less'ning vessel plows the foaming main;
She sighs, she calls, she waves the sign in vain.

GAY.

RETRANSLATION.

Let there roam on the desolate beach of Naxos
    The Cretan maid, left alone by her faithless suitor:
The breeze is sweeping her tresses dishevell'd, like one in-
      mourning:
    A token of grief, there falls many a tear.
Her spouse forsworn is spreading his treacherous canvas   5
    To catch the prosperous gales in white bosom.
"Turn thy bark, Theseus!" she cries aloud; "lull ye,
    ye winds!"
    Theseus is deafer even than the deaf south-wind.
A cliff stands near; in-distraction she makes-for the heights
    of the cliff,
    And gives well-known signals with waved hand.   10
But still the sailor cleaves the deep, ever more and more
    distant,
    And of no avail are tear (and) signals, (and) prayers.

HINTS.

1. "Let there roam," *fac* . . . *spatietur.*
2. "Cretan maid," *Gnôsis*. see xxvii 7
3. "Is sweeping," *rapit.*   "Like one in mourning," *lugentis more.*
5. "Canvas," pl.
6. "To catch," *quae* with subj.
7. "Lull ye." For the intransitive use of *pono*, applied to the winds, comp. Virg. *Aen.* vii. 27.
8. "Even," expressed by *ipse*, in agreement with *Theseus.*
10. Comp. Ov. *Her.* x. 40.
11. "Ever more and more," *jam jamque* with comparative

EXERCISE XXIX.

Hɪɢʜ blew the blast, the waves ran fast,
  The boat was overthrown,
And soon he saw his fair Annie
  Come floating in the foam.

He caught her by the yellow hair,
  And drew her up on the sand :
Fair Annie's corpse lay at his feet,
  And his young son came never to land.

"Oh wae to my cruel mother !
  An ill death may she dee !
She turn'd fair Annie frae my door,
  Wha died for love o' me."

RETRANSLATION.

The blasts sound hoarsely, and suddenly by the coursing
    waves

Overwhelmed, the boat founders in the midst of the sea.

Watching from land, the husband recognised borne through
    the waters

The fair limbs of his own wife.

No sooner seen, than seized (*acc.*) by the yellow locks to
    himself   5

He drew (her), and places his mournful burden on dry
    ground.

But though there lies before his feet the fair Neaera,

The beloved infant, a second care, is missing to his father.

"Ah ! for thy deserts, most ruthless mother," he cries,

    "May the gods grant thee to perish by a cruel death ! 10

For by thee was Neaera repelled from closed doors,

    Whom alas ! too faithful the gloomy day (of death) has
    carried off.

HINTS

1. "Hoarsely," *rauca*, adj. Note that in Latin an adjective is
often used to qualify a verb, in the way that we should do by an
adverb. Thus *laetus excepit*, "he welcomed him joyfully." See the
Public School Lat. Gr. (1883), p. 278. "Coursing." Comp. Virg.
Aen. v. 193, "Maleaeque *sequacibus* undis."

2. "Founders," *perit* "Sea," *gurgite*.

3. "Recognised," to come in line 4.

5. "No sooner . . than," *ut videt* . . *ut* This idiom gives
vividness to an expression, as in Virg. "Ut vidi, ut perii, ut me malus
abstulit error."

9. "Ah ! for," etc. Comp. Virg. *Aen.* ii. 535, "At tibi pro scelere,
exclamat, pro talibus ausis | Di," etc.

11. Begin with *occlusis etenim*, or *scilicet occlusis*.

EXERCISE XXX.

THE boatmen shout, " 'Tis time to part,
  No longer may we stay : "
'Twas then Matilda taught my heart
  How much a glance can say.

With trembling steps to me she came,
  Farewell ! she would have cried ;
But, ere her lips the word could frame,
  In half-form'd sounds it died.

Then bending down, with looks of love,
  Her arms she round me flung ;
And, as the gale hangs on the grove,
  Upon my breast she hung.

My willing arms embraced the maid,
  My heart with rapture beat ;
While she but wept the more, and said,
  " Would we had never met ! "

                        CARLYLE.

RETRANSLATION.

The sailors raise-a-shout : Now is it time to depart,
  The hour no longer admits-of delays for us.
At-once, what the expressiveness is of a look bent-upon-one,
  Beloved Delia taught my heart.
With uncertain steps she had started to come to me,   5
  And now wished to utter the (word) Farewell.

But ere she could frame (that) last word,

   The faint sounds died-away from her lips.

Then bending her head and her countenance flushed with
      love,

   She flung her outstretched arms round my neck.   10

And as at times a light breeze hangs on the wood,

   Even so does my love hang on my breast.

With-what-joy do my arms seize the maiden in an em
      brace ;

   My gladsome heart throbs with unwonted emotion.

Yet-none-the-less fills she her bosom with tears, and says : 15

   O ! would that no chance had united us as companions.

Hints.

3. " Bent-upon-me. Compare Virg. *Aen*. ii. 1, " *Intenti*que ora
tenebant."

5. " Had started to come."   Lit. " had advanced of her own
accord."   *Ultro* has often the force of " taking the initiative," " being
the first to," as in " Ultro animos tollit dictis atque increpat ultro,"
Aen. ix. 127.

6. " The (word)," *illud*.

7. " Ere."   The two parts of *prius-quam* or *ante-quam* may be
separated in Latin verse.

11. " Hangs," perf.

13. " With what joy," *quam laeta*.

14. " Gladsome."   Comp. Ov. *Fast*. iii. 523, " Idibus est Annae
festum *geniale* Perennae."

15. " Says," *ait*, to come at the end of line 16.   *o nos* will come
instead at the end of line 15.   For " had united " use the syncopated
form of the plup. subj. of the verb.

EXERCISE XXXI.

THE STORMY PETREL.

UP and down! up and down!
From the base of the waves to the billow's crown,
Amidst the flashing and feathery foam
The stormy petrel finds a home;
A home,—if such a place can be
For her who lives on the wide, wide sea,
On the craggy ice, in the frozen air,
And only seeking her rocky lair
To warn her young, and teach them to spring
At once o'er the waves on their stormy wing.

O'er the deep! o'er the deep!
Where the whale and the shark and the sword-fish sleep,
Outflying the blast and the driving rain,
The petrel telleth her tale in vain;
For the mariner curseth the warning bird,
Who bringeth him news of the storm unheard.

BARRY CORNWALL

RETRANSLATION.

Poised on the summit of the waves, anon of the depth the
      lowest
   Waters thou skimmest, hither and thither, harbinger of
      storm;

And 'tis thy pleasure amid the waves, where is scattered
    the whitening
Foam, to have fixed thy stormy abode.
A strange home! Does any care keep at home a bird   5
    That is ever wont to live amid the swelling waters?
For whom the rugged ice is a home, for whom the cold air,
    And who so seldom repairs-to her rocky dwelling.
Then she keeps-close-to her nestlings, a dutiful parent;
    then she teaches them
To scud over the azure seas in tempestuous career.   10
Where the sword-fish and the whale seek quiet repose,
    Do thou cleave through the deep waters an unceasing
    course.
Outstripping the winds, a bird swifter than the very storm-
    clouds,
    Pour forth thy warnings, never believed (*nom.*)
Though thou art a faithful harbinger of the coming storm, 15
    The sailor goes-his-way invoking curses on thy head.

HINTS.

1. "Poised," *pendens.* "Depth," *gurges.*
2. "Harbinger of storm," *hiemis nuntia.*
4. "Abode," *lăres (pl.)*
7. "Rugged," *aspera.*
9 "Keep close to," *foveo.*
    9, 10. The words in these lines are blended together. "Teaches"
comes at the end of 10, "seas" and "career" in 9.
11. "Sword-fish," *xĭphĭas,* a word found in *Ov. Halieut.* 97
14. "Never," *non unquam.*
16. "Invoking curses on," *dira precatus,* with *dat.*

EXERCISE XXXII.

DEAR is my little native vale,
  The ringdove builds and murmurs there ;
Close to my cot she tells her tale
  To every passing villager.
The squirrel leaps from tree to tree,
And shells his nuts at liberty.

Through orange groves and myrtle bowers,
  That breathe a gale of fragrance round,
I charm the fairy-footed hours
  With the loved lute's romantic sound ;
Or crowns of living laurel weave
For those that run the race at eve.

ROGERS.

RETRANSLATION.

Dear to me (are) the bounds of my native-place, the little
      valley ;
  Here the dove makes her nest, here murmuring coos.
Sitting near, hard by my dwelling, she repeats her complaint
    To the villagers, such as care to pass-by.
The squirrel leaps unharmed from branch to branch,   5
    And cracks nuts, no one hindering him.
Through a grove blushing with apples of Alcinous and with
      myrtle,
    Whence a sweet fragrance swells widely flowing,

Tuning a Lesbian strain on the loved lute,
　　I beguile the time (*pl.*) gliding with soft step,   10
Or else weave the prizes of the race at-evening (*adj.*),
　　That garlands of-bay be not wanting to the locks of the
　　　young.

Hints.

1. "Bounds," *confinia.*
2. "Murmuring coos," *rauca . . . gemit.*
3. "Near," *vicina.*　"Repeats," *recinit.*
4. "Such as care," *si cui . . . libet.*　Use the perf. inf. for "pass by."
5. "Squirrel," *sciurus* (the "bushy-tailed").　A short vowel must be allowed before this word, as it could not otherwise be brought into the verse.

"Hindering," *praepediente.*

7. Notice this equivalent for "orange groves," and compare Virg. *Georg.* ii. 87, "Pomaque et Alcinoi silvae."　Pliny has *arbor Mēdica* for the orange or citron tree.

8. "Swells," *abundat.*

9. "Lesbian," *Lesbōum.*　For "lute," *plectrum* may be used, being literally the quill or instrument with which the strings were struck.

EXERCISE XXXIII.

WEAVE thee a wreath of woodbine, child,
　　'Twill suit thy infant brow ;
It runs up free in the woodlands wild,
　　As tender, as frail as thou.

He bound his brow with a woodbine wreath,
　　And smiled his playful eye,
And he softly skipp'd o'er the blossom'd heath,
　　In his young heart's ecstasy.

I saw him not till his manly brow
  Was clouded with thought and care,
And the smile of youth and its beauty now
  No longer wanton'd there.

Go, twine thee a crown of the ivy-tree,
  And gladden thy loaded breast;
Bright days may yet shine out for thee,
  And thy bosom again know rest.

LONGFELLOW.

RETRANSLATION.

Let the trailing woodbine weave thee garlands, child,
  Such garlands will suit thy brow;
That flower amid the uncultivated recesses of the forest
    spontaneously
  Shoots up, and, tender itself, resembles thee frail.

The boy bound his brow with such a chaplet,   5
  And a becoming smile was on the face of (him) playing,
Then he danced gently amid the fragrant heather
  Exulting, while his merry bosom throbbed.

Years went by; at length under manly forehead
  Was a gloomy brow and gloomy care: 10
Alas! the boyish laughter had fled from that countenance,
  Nor does the early gracefulness hover round his head.

Go! bind thy brow now with clinging ivy,
  At length about-to-lay-aside the load of anxiety;
Perhaps the day about-to-come will shine more brightly, 15
  And rest will again soothe thy wearied breast.

HINTS.

1. "Woodbine." No word exactly expressing this is to be :
the Latin poets. Linnaeus uses *lonicera*, which is not a classi
at all. As *periclymenus* is found in Pliny, and also (as a prop·
in Ovid, it is perhaps the most eligible.

3. "That" (of yours), *iste.*

7 "Gently," *lenis.* See note on xxix. 1.

10. "Brow," *supercilium.*

13. "Go," *en age.* "Clinging," *sequax.*

EXERCISE XXXIV.

HE left his home with a swelling sail,
  Of fame and fortune dreaming ;
With a spirit as free as the vernal gale,
  Or the pennon above him streaming.

He hath reach'd his goal : by a distant wave,
  'Neath a sultry sun they've laid him ;
And stranger forms bent o'er his grave,
  When the last sad rites were paid him.

He should have died in his own loved land,
  With friends and kinsmen near him,
Nor have wither'd thus on a foreign strand,
  With no thought, save heaven, to cheer him

RETRANSLATION.

How joyful did the swelling sails bear him away fro
        country !
What honour and what great wealth did he antic

As free in heart as the pennons that from the top of the
   Mast stream, or as the vernal breeze flies on.
See the end of his journey! by the waves of a distant
     shore,
                                                   5
Beneath a burning sun, they have laid the hero to rest.
Nay more, while his corse is receiving its last honour,
   A foreign race of men thronging-round looks on.
He ought to have breathed out his life in his native land,
   Where a friendly hand close-by might bring solace,   10
And not thus on a foreign shore his fading life to have
   Laid down, where the only hope remaining is in heaven.

Hints.

3. "As the pennons," etc.   Lit. "as the pennons (*insignia*) do *not*
stream, etc., *nor* the vernal breeze fly on."   The negative in the second
clause of the comparison appears in English by turning the sentence
the other way about · "The streaming pennons are *not* so free as he."
"From," *de*, to begin line 4.

6. "Lay to rest," *compono*.

7. "Nay more," *quin et*, or *quinetiam*.   "Is receiving," lit.
"enjoys."

8. "Foreign,"*alienus*.   The same word in line 11 will be rendered
by *externus*.   "Looks on," *videt*.

9. "He ought to have," etc.   *Debuerat*, with pres. inf.

11. "And not," *nec*.   "To have laid down," pres. inf. for the
same reason as in line 9.

12. "Where," etc., lit. "where the only hope remains."   For
"heaven," use *Elӯsium*.

EXERCISE XXXV.

(The same continued.)

BUT what recks it now ? is his sleep less sound
    In the port where the wild waves swept him,
Than if home's green turf his grave had bound,
    Or the hearts he loved had wept him ?

Then why repine ?   Can he feel the rays
    That pestilent sun sheds o'er him ?
Or share the grief that may cloud the days
    Of the friends who now deplore him ?

No! his bark's at anchor; its sails are furled ;
    It hath 'scaped the storm's deep chiding ;
And safe from the buffeting waves of the world
    By a haven of peace is riding.

ALARIC WATTS.

RETRANSLATION.

What matters it ? for not closed in less deep slumber
    Are his eyes there, where the light breeze has born
        him,
Than if his own soil had bound (him) with the familia
        turf,
    And his own (friends) had performed the last sa
        funeral rites.

Whence then (is) repining ?   Will *he* feel the heats,   5
     Although the sun weighs-on those regions with pesti-
          lential force ?
When the loss (*pl.*) weighs-on these friends that now feel
          pity,
     Will he also weep, touched by the woes of his friends ?
Not so : the anchor holds his ship with its sails furled ;
     The chiding of the hoarse-sounding wind is hushed :   10
He himself, long tost on the troublesome billows of the
          world,
     Has escaped, and is enjoying rest in tranquil waters.

HINTS.

1. What is the difference between *rĕfert* and *rēfert ?*   "For not,"
neque enim.

3. "Soil," *tellus.*

4. "Funeral rites," pl. of *funus.*

5. "He" (emphat.), *ille.*

6. "Weighs on," *premat* (subj. after *licet*).

9. "Furled," *compositis.*

10. "Chiding," *jurgia* (pl)

11. "The world," *res* (pl.)

12. "Rest," *otia* (pl.)

EXERCISE XXXVI.

THE GRAVES OF A HOUSEHOLD.

THEY grew in beauty side by side,
     They fill'd one home with glee ;
Their graves are sever'd, far and wide,
     By mount, and stream, and sea.

G

The same fond mother bent at night
  O'er each fair sleeping brow;
She had each folded flower in sight;
  Where are those dreamers now?

One, midst the forests of the west,
  By a dark stream is laid;
The Indian knows his place of rest,
  Far in the cedar shade.

The sea, the blue lone sea, hath one;
  He lies where pearls lie deep;
He was the loved of all, yet none
  O'er his low bed may weep.

RETRANSLATION.

They grew together, beautiful in the bloom of youth;
  One home resounded with (their) joyous laughter (*pl.*)
But now, alas! mountain and streams and the sea
  Have parted their graves in different places.
For them the same mother, as often as night had laid their
      limbs to rest,   5
  Bent yearningly over the slumbering brows:
She was carefully tending them, like closed flowers:—
  Oh! where are (they) whose gentle rest that was?
Where America spreads its boundless woodlands, the eldest
  Sank down: a dark stream flows-past his bones.   10
The wandering Indians know his grave;
  The secluded cedar overshadows his resting-place.
The sea overwhelmed one beneath its azure waters,
  Where many a gem lies-hidden in the lonely deep:

He had been dear to all while life remained ; 15
   (But) to none is it given to shed tears over his remains.

HINTS.

3, 4. "And the sea," to begin line 4 ; "graves" to end line 3. "Have parted," *distinuere.*

5. "Lay to rest," *sterno.*

6. "Yearningly," *inhians.* This line will end with a quadrisyllable.

7. "Tend," *recolo.* The word may have the sense of "mentally reckoning up," as in Virg. *Aen.* vi. 681.

9. "America," *Amĕrīca.* Begin with *maximus* (*natu* understood).

10. "Dark," *niger,* allowed to end the pentameter for emphasis.

12. "Resting-place," *funeream . . . humum.*

13. "One," *est quem.* For "waters" here use *marmor* (sing.)

14. "Many a," *plurima.*

16. "Shed tears over," *illacrimo,* with dative.

EXERCISE XXXVII.

(*The same continued.*)

ONE sleeps where southern vines are drest
   Above the noble slain :
He wrapt his colours round his breast
   On a blood-red field of Spain.

And one—o'er her the myrtle showers
   Its leaves, by soft winds fann'd ;
She faded midst Italian flowers,
   The last of that bright band.

And parted thus they rest, who play'd
   Beneath the same green tree,

Whose voices mingled as they pray'd
  Around one parent knee ;

They that with smiles lit up the hall,
  And cheer'd with song the hearth :—
Alas ! for love, if thou wert all,
  And nought beyond, oh earth !

Mrs. Hemans.

RETRANSLATION.

The third, where they dress in order the Spanish vines,
  And the gallant soldier enriches the soil with his blood,
Wrapt his breast in-death with his country's flag,
  Where the fields are red enriched with torrents of blood.
Yet one (*fem.*) remains, whom the myrtle with its leaves
      to strew   5
  Ever loves, the zephyr scarce stirring its foliage.
She faded drooping amid Italian flowers,
  Destined-to-perish the last member of the bright band.
And so they lie separated ; whom and whose countless
      jests,
  In their merriment, one tree had sheltered with its
      leaves,   10
And who used once to pray-to God with blended voices,
  (While) their mother herself had bent the knee in their
      midst.
Their home seemed itself to return the laughter of the
      children ;
  The hearth to grow ever more joyful with their songs.
Alas ! how idle (would be) love, if nought remained to the
      loving-one ;   15
  If thou, O short-lived earth, wert all to the unhappy !

HINTS.

1. "Dress," *tondent*.
2. "Gallant," *nobilis*.
4. "Torrents of," *multus*.
6. " Stirring," abl. absol.
8. "Member," *pars*.

9, 10. These lines are blended together in the Latin.   End line 9 with *frondibus arbor*.   "And whose countless jests, in their merriment," *innumerosque hilarum . . . jocos*, in line 10.

16. "Wert," *fores*.

EXERCISE XXXVIII.

CORONACH.

HE is gone on the mountain,
   He is lost to the forest,
Like a summer-dried fountain,
   When our need was the sorest.
The font reappearing
   From the rain-drops shall borrow ;
But to us comes no cheering,
   To Duncan no morrow.

The hand of the reaper
   Takes the ears that are hoary,
But the voice of the weeper
   Wails manhood in glory.
The autumn winds rushing
   Waft the leaves that are searest ;
But our flower was in flushing
   When blighting was nearest.

RETRANSLATION.

'Tis done : not again will he traverse the mountain's tops,
   Not again will he chase the wild-boars in the forests.
As when a fountain is dried-up in the summer rising of
      the dog-star,
   He perishes in the mid tide of our cares.
The fountain welling-out again will come forth to the
      upper air,   5
   And a friendly shower will supply fresh waters.
But alas ! no consolation will come for our grief,
   For Duncan no morrow is destined-to-arise.
The reaper puts his sickle to the ripe corn,
   And only the whitening ear falls beneath his blade ; 10
But we sigh with tears for a comrade taken-away,
   For whom the prime of age was not impaired.
If at times the south wind has-let-loose its gales at the
      rising of Arcturus,
   The anger of the blast sweeps-off the leaves that-are-
      dry.
But our (comrade) was glowing with the early bloom of
      youth,   15
   When the hurried day of destruction was at hand.

HINTS.

3. Comp. Tibull. i. 1. 27, "Sed Canis aestivos ortus vitare sub umbra."

4. "Tide," *aestus* (pl.) Comp. Hor. *Sat.* i. 2. 110.

5. "Air," *aura* (pl.)

8. "Duncan." This can either be Latinized into *Duncānus*, or some classical name chosen, as *Dēmŏlĕos* or *Eurўălus*. Care must be taken in such a case not to choose a name with incongruous associations. The former for his prowess ("qui cursu palantes Troas

agebat "), the latter for his death in the bloom of youth, might seem not unsuitable.

9. " Corn," *arista*, lit. the awn or beard of the ear.

10. " And only," *nec nisi*.

11. " With tears," *flentes*.   " Sigh for," *suspiro* (acc.)

12. " Prime," *honor*.

13. " At the rising of," *sub*, with acc.   For the rest of the line comp. Tibull. i. 1. 47, " Aut gelidas hibernus aquas cum fuderit Auster."

14. " That are dry," *arentes*.

16. " Hurried," *properata*.

EXERCISE XXXIX.

(*The same continued.*)

FLEET foot on the correi,
  Sage counsel in cumber,
Red hand in the foray,
  How sound is thy slumber !
Like the dew on the mountain,
  Like the foam on the river,
Like the bubble on the fountain,
  Thou art gone, and for ever !

SCOTT.

RETRANSLATION.

Thou who with swift footstep didst scour the secluded
    lairs of wild beasts,
  And, when Mars was harassing, didst give sagacious
    counsel,

Who didst bring back a right hand blood-stained from
 slaughter of enemies,
Fallest ; and thee laid-low deep repose now holds.
As dews on the mountain vanish at the rising of the sun, 5
 As foam sparkles on the river and suddenly perishes,
As a bubble, when at times it swells on a glassy fount,
 Demoleus departs, not to be recalled by us.

HINTS

 1. "Secluded lairs," etc., *stabula alta ferarum* (Virg.) A *correi* is
a hollow on a hill-side where the game lodges.
 3. "Of enemies," *hostili*.
 5. "At," *in*.
 6. "Suddenly," *repens*. Note the difference between *rĕpens* and
rēpens.

EXERCISE XL.

HOME they brought her warrior dead .
 She nor swoon'd, nor utter'd cry :
All her maidens, watching, said,
 " She must weep or she will die."

Then they praised him, soft and low,
 Call'd him worthy to be loved,
Truest friend and noblest foe,
 Yet she neither spoke nor moved.

Stole a maiden from her place,
 Lightly to the warrior stept,
Took the face-cloth from the face :
 Yet she neither moved nor wept.

Rose a nurse of ninety years,
  Set his child upon her knee—
Like summer tempest came her tears—
  "Sweet my child, I live for thee."

TENNYSON.

RETRANSLATION.

Lo! they bring-back home her husband slain in war!
  She (says) nothing, nor does a rigid shudder come-over
    her frame.
Anxious and marvelling her maidens watch:
  "If she weep not, she will not long be among the living."

Then with suppressed murmur each one praises the pros-
    trate one,   5
  Worthy indeed, worthy that one should love him, he
    was:
A hero, than whom no other (was) more noble; to the
    foeman a resolute
  Foeman; in friendship steadfast:" but she (spake)
    nothing.

A handmaid goes-forth from the line in which the rest are
    standing around.
  Daring to approach the corpse with light step: 10
She goes-to the warrior: his face is shrouded with a cloth:
  She draws-away the covering from his countenance: yet
    she (says) nothing.

There rises an aged woman, who had seen ninety years,
  And she placed his child on the mother's knee.
Then tears burst-forth like a summer tempest:—   15
  "Dear one, I live for thee! thou (art) left for me," she
    says.

HINTS.

2. "Shudder." Comp. Virg. *Aen.* ii. 121, "gelidusque per ima cucurrit ossa *tremor.*" Or the sentence might be turned : "nor does the accustomed warmth quit her frame." Comp. Virg. *Aen.* iv. 705, ix. 475.

6. "Worthy indeed," *dignus enim,* followed by the relative and impft. subj. For this sense of *enim,* comp. Virg. *Aen.* x. 874, "Aeneas agnovit enim," and "tibi enim, tibi maxima Juno."

10. Another turn might be : "And with timid footstep approaches where he lies."

11. "Cloth," *vestis.*

13. "Ninety." As *nonaginta* would be a heavy word, turn by "ten times nine," or "nine times ten," using the distributive form of the numeral.

14. "And placed," *deposuitque.* Usually *que* should be the second word in the sentence, but to ease the restraints of the pentameter, it is sometimes allowed after a long verb in the second half, as here. Comp. Ov. *Fast.* vi. 84, "Romulus, in partes distribuitque suas." For "child," *sobolem* may be used, as there is nothing to show whether boy or girl is meant. In the last line, the gender must be shown, and may be left to the composer's choice.

15. "Like," *more,* with genitive.

16. "Left," in the sense of "saved," *sospĕs.*

EXERCISE XLI.

As thro' the land at eve we went,
    And pluck'd the ripen'd ears,
We fell out, my wife and I,
O we fell out I know not why,
    And kiss'd again with tears.

> And blessings on the falling out
>   That all the more endears,
> When we fall out with those we love,
> . And kiss again with tears !
> For when we came where lies the child
>   We lost in other years,
> There above the little grave,
> O there above the little grave,
>   We kiss'd again with tears.
>
>   TENNYSON.

RETRANSLATION.

While lately at even we roam-through the cornfields,
  Plucking the proffered wheat-ears with united hand,
Between us bound in marriage there intervened a rising
        dissension ;
  But love renewed kisses mingled with tears.
And blessings on the quarrel which separates lovers, in
        such wise   5
  That there ensues from it in turn a stronger attachment.
If it chance that discord has severed the affections of two,
  How sweet it is to shed mutual tears on tender bosom !
For as soon as we came where laid in earth the infant
  Was, snatched from us in time past,   10
Standing by the little mound, new pledges to our vows
  We add, and kisses with mingled tears.

HINTS.

1. "Cornfields," *segetes* . . . *et arva*, by hendiadys.
2. "Proffered wheat-ears," *spicea dona*.
5. "Blessings on," *bene sit*, with dative.

6. "In turn," *alternis* (sc. *vicibus*), as often in Lucretius.

7. "If it chance that," *si forte*. The words need not begin the line.

8. "To shed mutual tears," *mutua flere*. Compare Lucret. ii. 75. So Virgil uses *per mutua, Aen.* vii. 66.

9. "We came," *ventum est*

12. "Tears," *lacrimulis*. The choice of the diminutive, and the four-syllable ending, gives to the line the tone of one from Catullus, in harmony with the general style of the subject. Comp. Catull. lxvi. 16.

EXERCISE XLII.

ETON.

LONG tost on Fortune's waves, I come to rest,
Eton, once more on thy maternal breast.
On loftiest deeds to fix the aspiring gaze,
To seek the purer lights of ancient days,
To love the simple paths of manly truth :—
These were thy lessons to my opening youth.
If on my later life some glory shine,
Some honour grace my name, the meed is thine.
My boyhood's nurse, my aged dust receive,
And one last tear of kind remembrance give.

 EARL OF DERBY.

RETRANSLATION.

Harassed by the shifting waves of fortune and affairs,
    I return too-late to thy bosom, Eton.

To follow great (objects) and to admire the heights of lofty
 fame,
 And to approach the pure ray of ancient light,
I learnt (as) a boy under thy guidance; and at life's
 threshold   5
 To love the honourable paths of true merit.
If in life's decline any glory my name
 Has adorned, or any distinction has ennobled,
'Tis thy gift, kindly-one. Grant a sepulchre, fostering
 earth;
 Grant a last tear, and (one) mindful of me.   10

HINTS.

2. " Eton," *Ĕtŏna.*

3. "Great objects," neut. pl. of adjective.

5. "Under thy guidance," *auspice te.*   In this line the sense runs
on from the preceding pentameter.   As a rule this should be avoided.

6. "Merit." *Laus* has sometimes this meaning, as in *Aen.* ix. 522,
" pro laudibus istis."

8. "Has adorned." Use the future perfect for the verbs in this
line.   In case of the second the syncopated form (*-ārit* for *-āverit*) will
be requisite.

9. "'Tis thy gift." *Muneris . . . tui est.*   Comp. Ov. *Met.*, xiv.
125.

EXERCISE XLIII.

GENERAL GORDON.

WARRIOR of God, man's friend, not here below,
 But somewhere dead far in the waste Soudan,
Thou livest in all hearts, for all men know
 This earth hath borne no simpler, nobler man.

TENNYSON.

RETRANSLATION.

Soldier ! lover of men, not here, godlike one, dost thou rest :
    The sand of Meroe covers thee, far-away, released-from-
        service.
Thou remainest a single love for all—all have one voice :—
    " None was more simple or more noble."

HINTS.

1. "Rest," *recumbis.*

2. "Of Meroe," *Mĕrŏēs.* "Released from service," of a soldier who
has gained his discharge, *emeritus.*

3. "All have," *omnibus . . . est.* The line ends with an elision
before *est.*

EXERCISE XLIV.

THE ALMA.

THOUGH till now ungraced in story, scant although thy
    waters be,
Alma, roll those waters proudly, proudly roll them to the sea.
Yesterday unnamed, unhonoured, but to wandering Tartar
    known,
Now thou art a voice for ever, to the world's four quarters
    blown.
In two nations' annals graven, thou art now a deathless name,
And a star for ever shining in their firmament of fame.
Many a great and ancient river, crowned with city, tower,
    and shrine,
Little streamlet, knows no magic, boasts no potency like
    thine ;

Cannot shed the light thou sheddest around many a living
    head,
Cannot lend the light thou lendest to the memories of the
    dead.

RETRANSLATION.

Though thou art scanty, and not yet made mention of, Alma,
    Yet to-day thou rollest illustrious waters into the sea.
Thee, save some Scythian wayfarer wandering through
        the wilds,
    Yesterday no one saw : thou wert nothing save a name.
But to-day by her voice through all ages thee   5
    Over sea, over lands, favourable renown will bear.
The annals that Gaul and that England writes
    Tell-of thee ; thou sparklest a shining star for both.
Grant that many a stream upbears splendid cities,
    Yet it yields in magic, little rivulet, to thee.   10
For, as though thou wert ever encircled with a great
        contest,
    O rivulet, thou charmest the feeling hearts of men.

HINTS.

3. "The wilds," *aperta* (neut. pl.); lit. "the open country."

7. "And that ;" express by repeating *quos scribit*, with the order of
words reversed, to mark the antithesis.

9. "Grant that," *si* with the indic. When *si* takes this mood, the
condition is assumed as a fact. Hence it may then be often rendered
"since."

10. "In magic," *arte.*

12. "Charmest," *delenis.* To avoid the use of *rivule* for "O rivulet"
(on which see the Preface), begin with *Tu pia,* and insert *rive* in the
second part of the line. So, in line 10, *parvule rive* may be used instead of the more tempting *rivule parve.*

EXERCISE XLV.

(*The same continued.*)

YEA, nor all unsoothed their sorrow, who can, proudly
   mourning, say,
When the first strong burst of anguish shall have wept
   itself away :
" He has past from us, the loved one ; but he sleeps with
   them that died
By the Alma, at the winning of that terrible hill-side."
Yea, and in the days far onward, when we all are cold as those
Who beneath thy vines and willows on their hero-beds repose,
Thou, on England's banners blazoned with the famous
   fields of old,
Shalt, where other fields are winning, wave above the
   brave and bold :
And our sons unborn shall nerve them for some great deed
   to be done
By that twentieth of September, when the Alma's heights
   were won.
O thou river, dear for ever to the gallant, to the free,
Alma, roll thy waters proudly, proudly roll them to the sea.
                                                      TRENCH.

RETRANSLATION.

And with some consolation does he soothe the plaintive
   mind,
   When grief has passed-away with a sudden gush (of
   tears) from the eyes,

Who, sorrowfully exulting, shall be able to say : " I shall
    see
  " Thee never, brother more to-be-beloved than life ;
" But thou reclinest a hero and among heroes by the
    Alma,   5
  " Having dared to climb the ridge of the deadly hill-side."
And when we also are stiff in the cold of death,
    As (they) whom the vine there covers and the gray
    willow,
Thy name, Alma, shall adorn the standards of Britons,
    Stirring the brave hearts of men to fresh deeds.   10
And (the child) yet unborn, mindful of the month and day,
    Will perform a great achievement, fighting for his
    country.
O Alma, dear to large-hearted and to brave men,
    Proudly roll thy waves into the sea !

HINTS.

1. "Some," *non nullus ;* "and . . . some," *nec nullus.*   These
forms should be remembered, as also *nullus non,* "every."

2. "Has passed away," *cesserit.*   "Gush," *imber.*

3. "To say," *dixisse.*   For the tense comp. Hor. *Ars Poet.* 328.

4. "More to be beloved," *amabilior,* allowed to end the line for
emphasis.

5. "Heroes," acc. pl. *hērōās.*

6. "Ridge," *colla* (n. pl.)

8. "Gray," lit. "white," *alba.*

9 "Of Britons," *Britannum* (contracted gen. plur.)

12. "Achievement," *opus.*

14. "Proudly," *exsultans.*

EXERCISE XLVI.

ODE.

UPLIFT a thousand voices full and sweet
    In this wide hall, with earth's inventions stored,
    And praise th' invisible, universal Lord,
Who lets once more in peace the nations meet,
    Where Science, Art, and Labour have outpour'd
Their myriad horns of plenty at our feet.

O silent father of our kings to be,
Mourn'd in this golden hour of jubilee,
For this, for all, we weep our thanks to thee!

RETRANSLATION.

Uplift together a thousand voices and sounding applause,
    Where this floor houses the treasures conveyed-together;
Praising the One Deity, visible to none,
    Who suffers the peoples again to meet-together in peace,
Where Labour and Skill joined to Art its handmaid,   5
    Have poured the full horns at our feet.
And thou, silent father of the race to which thou hast given
    the sceptre,
    Whom the hour of rejoicing (though) golden yet grieves-
    for,
These things too, (and) many things also due to thee,
    weeping
    We look-back-upon, and continue thy praises.   10

HINTS.

2. "Floor," *area*, lit. "threshing-floor."

6. "Horns," *i.e.* "of plenty," *cornua* (*copiae* being understood).

7. "Sceptre," plural.

9. "Due," *non indebita*   A qualifying word may often, as here, be expressed by the negation of its opposite, as *haud raro = saepe*, *non nunquam* nearly = *interdum*.   Observe that while *non nunquam* means "sometimes," *nunquam non* means "always."   So with regard to *non nullus* and *nullus non*.

10. "Continue," *prosequimur*, lit. "follow forth."

EXERCISE XLVII.

(*The same continued.*)

O YE, the wise who think, the wise who reign,
From growing commerce loose her latest chain,
And let the fair, white-wing'd peacemaker fly
To happy havens under all the sky,
And mix the seasons and the golden hours,

    Till each man find his own in all men's good,
    Till all men work in noble brotherhood,
Breaking their mailed fleets and armed towers,
And ruling by obeying nature's powers ;
And gathering all the fruits of peace, and crown'd with
    all her flowers.

TENNYSON.

RETRANSLATION.

Ye also, to whom the gods have given intelligence, to
    whom (they have given) sovereignty,
Loose now the bonds of fresh commerce ;

And through all havens and prosperous homes
  Let the fair harbinger of coming peace go.
So let a golden season bring happy hours,   5
  And the power of seeing another's good in one's own;
That (men) may learn, their fleets being broken and their
     arms put-away,
  To associate every-one in their own fraternity.
Obey ye nature: he rules who obeys; and the stores (*acc.*)
  Of peace have ye (*imper.*) and the glory of an undying
     flower.   10

Hints.

1. "To whom," *queis.* "Sovereignty" may be turned by the pres. infin. of *regno.* This is really a verbal noun, as in Persius's "Usque adeone | Scire tuum nihil est, nisi te scire hoc sciat alter."

2. "Fresh." The adjective, being emphatical, may stand at the end of the pentameter, as in "Bulbus et ex horto quae venit herba salax;" but this licence must be taken very sparingly.

4. "Coming," fut. participle.

6. "The power of seeing," *posse videre.* See note on ver. 1.

8. "Everyone," *quemque.*

*** Note in this version how the lines are transposed—3 and 4, and 8 and 9, and try to see the reason. "Nuntia pacis" would probably occur as the natural equivalent of "peacemaker," and "nuntia pacis eat" as an appropriate ending for the pentameter; while the words for "happy havens," being spondaic, were more fitted for the hexameter. So with the others.

EXERCISE XLVIII.

MY life is like the summer rose,
  That opens to the morning sky,
But, ere the shades of evening close,
  Is scatter'd on the ground to die.

But on that rose's humble bed
The sweetest dews of night are shed,
As if Heav'n wept such waste to see :—
But none shall weep a tear for me.

My life is like the autumnal leaf
    That trembles in the moon's pale ray ;
Its hold is frail, its date is brief,
    Restless, and soon to pass away.
Yet, ere that leaf shall fall or fade,
The parent tree shall mourn its shade.
The winds bewail the leafless tree,
But none shall breathe a sigh for me.

RETRANSLATION.

My life (is) like a rose in the first season of summer,
    That blushes, opened by the morning sun,
But, as soon as Hesperus has drawn the shades of
        night over the earth,
    The flower fades soon-to-die on its native glebe.
But where the rose cut-down is strewn on a lowly bed,
    The ground is moist with the fragrant dew of night ;
As if the powers wept to behold the downfall :—
    But for me when-dead no tear-drop falls.
My life is like an autumn leaf in a garden,
    That quivers, struck by the flickering light of the
        moon ;
'Tis short-lived, 'tis frail, ill supported on its parent
        bough ;
    It cannot remain still, and already trembles ready-
        to-fall.

But if the leaf perish, if its beauty be smitten down,
    Its shade is not unwept by its parent;
The winds too bewail the bough bereft of its leaves :—15
    (Neither) love nor friendly mind will sigh for me.

HINTS.

1. Begin with *Vita mihi qualis.*
3. "Has drawn . . . over," fut. perf. of *induco* with dat.
4. "Soon to die" (fut. partic.)
8. "When dead," *exstincto.* "No," *non . . . ulla.*
10. "Struck," lit. "shaken," *quassa.*
12. "Remain still," *stare loco.*
13. "Beauty," *honores.*
16. Begin with *suspirabit. Nec* is understood with the first of the two nominatives.

EXERCISE XLIX.

(The same continued.)

MY life is like the print that feet
    Have left on Zara's desert strand.
Soon as the rising tide shall beat,
    The track shall vanish from the sand.

Yet, as if grieving to efface
    All vestige of the human race,
On that lone shore loud moans the sea :—
    But none shall e'er lament for me.

                                        R. H. WILDE.

RETRANSLATION.

My life is as the traces of a footstep far-apart,
  Which are-to-be-seen printed on Sarra's dry shore;
As soon as the wave rising-again strikes the sandy shore,
  Then there will be no mark of mortal foot.
But as though it sighed that utterly effaced should perish
  The signs of the human race, and should not be on the
    ground,
There resounds on the desert shore a deep moan from the
    waves :—
  (But) no complaint of my lot is heard.

HINTS.

1 "Far apart," *rarae.*
2. "Are to be seen," *patent.*   "Printed," *pressa.*
6. Begin the line with *gentis.*   "Should be," *fore.*

EXERCISE L.

Our life hangs by a single thread;
Soon 'tis cut, and we are dead.
Then boast not, reader, of thy might—
Alive at morn, and dead at night.
          Epitaph at Tunbridge Wells.

RETRANSLATION.

The life of men depends for us on a single thread;
  Straightway, when it is broken, we are turned to dust.

And so, reader, boast not thyself strong in vigour ;
  For at morn safe-and-sound, at night thou wilt be a
    corpse.

HINTS.

2. "When (it) is broken," *abrupto*.   "We are turned to dust," lit.
"are dust and a shadow ;" comp. Hor. *Carm.* IV. 7. 16.
  4. "Safe and sound," *sospes*.

EXERCISE LI.

LIKE crowded forest trees we stand,
  And some are mark'd to fall ;
The axe will smite at God's command,
  And soon shall smite us all.

Green as the bay-tree, ever green
  With its new foliage on,
The gay, the thoughtless have I seen :—
  I pass'd, and they were gone.

Read, ye that run, the awful truth
  With which I charge my page ;
A worm is in the bud of youth,
  And at the root of age.

                              COWPER.

RETRANSLATION.

Just as in the forests the pine-trees stand in close order,
  And, for those-that-are-to-fall, its own mark is traced on
    each,

So over us the axe ready-to-strike by divine command
  Hangs, and will soon consign every head to death.
Often have I seen men, who were flourishing in early age, 5
  As the bay-tree flourishes covered with new leaves ;
I have seen them free-from-care give time to foolish sport:—
  I passed by : the idle throng was nowhere.
Read, thou that runnest ; 'tis no long delay to thee reading ;
  Read the truths that my page contains :   10
A gnawing worm lurks, alas ! beneath the flower of rosy
          youth,
  And old age perishes, eaten at the root by a worm.

HINTS.

2. "For those that are to fall," *casuris*. "Traced," lit. "smeared," *illita*.

7. "Free from care," *securus*. Mark the difference between this and *tutus*.

8 "Idle," *frivola*.

9. "Read," lit. "read through," *perlege*.

10. "Page," *libellus*, lit. "small book." "Truths," *vera* (n. pl.)

12. "At the root," acc. of nearer definition.

EXERCISE LII.

To a Mountain Daisy.

Wee, modest, crimson-tipped flower
Thou's met me in an evil hour,
For I maun crush amang the stoure
                    Thy slender stem ;
To spare thee now is past my power,
                    Thou bonnie gem.

Alas ! it's no thy neebor sweet,
The bonnie lark, companion meet,
Bending thee 'mang the dewy weet,
               Wi' spreckled breast,
When upward springing, blithe to greet
               The purpling east.

Cauld blew the bitter-biting north
Upon thy early humble birth ;
Yet cheerfully thou glinted forth
               Amid the storm,
Scarce reared above the parent earth
               Thy tender form.

RETRANSLATION.

Tiny flower, adorned with rosy tints, an hour
   Ill-omened has brought thee to my sight ;
Straightway the plough will crush-through thy slender
    root,
   Nor, though wishing to spare, is the power granted to me.
Not the lark, thy sweet companion, denizen of the country, 5
   Is lightly pressing thee with dappled breast,
While the dew-drop glistens on the blooming field,
   And its soaring wing challenges the new-born day.
The northern blast was rough with pitiless storm,
   The ground was stiff, bound with wintry cold ;   10
But thee unharmed the heavy sleet of winter was fostering,
   And thy native earth upreared thy head.

HINTS.

1. " Tiny," *parvule.* The word for " adorned " will also be in the vocative.

3. "Straightway," *haud mora*. There are many useful phrases
mora, as *rumpe moras, tolle moras, posita mora*, etc.
4. "To me, though wishing," *licet optanti*. The infinitive of *p*
will express "the power."
5. "Denizen of," *quae servat*.
11. "Sleet," *imber*.

EXERCISE LIII.

(*The same continued.*)

THE flaunting flowers our gardens yield
High sheltering woods and wa's maun shield ;
But thou, beneath the random bield
                       O' clod or stane,
Adorns the histie stibble-field
                       Unseen, alane.

There in thy scanty mantle clad,
Thy snawy bosom upward spread,
Thou lift'st thy unassuming head
                       In humble guise ;
But now the share upturns thy bed,
                       And low thou lies.

Such is the fate of artless maid,
Sweet floweret of the rural shade,
By love's simplicity betrayed
                       And guileless trust ;
Till she, like thee, all soil'd is laid
                       Low i' the dust.

E'en thou who mourn'st the daisy's fate,
That fate is thine, no distant date ;
Stern ruin's ploughshare drives elate
            Full on thy bloom,
Till crush'd beneath the furrow's weight
            Shall be thy doom.
                BURNS.

RETRANSLATION.

A wall defends the lilies in a bright garden,
    And the holm-oak's shade screens them from the cold
       winds ;
But thou adornest the field, exposed in the midst of the
       herbage,
    And not seen by the eye of the passer-by.
And there lowly, and covered with thy slender mantle,
       thou   5
    Barest thy white bosom to the summer ray ;
Yet it avails thee nought to have lain-hid on lowly couch :
    Alas ! thou reclinest on the ground the prey of the hard
       ploughshare.
So, as often as the lovely offspring of the country,
    The maiden, lies betrayed by her own simplicity,   10
She falls, cast down by a like fate ; and no longer (of her)
       in the dark
    Dust reclining does any care remain.
And thou who bewailest in song the doom of the little
       flower,
    Thou too wilt fall cast down by a like fate ;
Dark ruin will crush with its ploughshare thee and thy
       flower,   15
    Straightway about-to-overwhelm thee in its own furrows.

HINTS.

1. " Bright," *purpureus*.   Horace even uses the word as an epithet of *olores*, swans.

3. " Exposed," *projectus*.   The word for " field " will come at the end of line 4.

5. " Covered," *adopertus*.   Begin the line with *Tuque*.

6. " Bosom," *pectora*.

10 " Betrayed," *prodita*, to begin line 9.

11. " Fate," *sorte*, to begin the line.

EXERCISE LIV.

SIGNS OF RAIN.

THROUGH the clear stream the fishes rise,
And nimbly catch the incautious flies.
The glow-worms, numerous and bright,
Illumed the dewy dell last night.
At dusk the squalid toad was seen
Hopping and crawling o'er the green.
The whirling wind the dust obeys,
And in the rapid eddy plays.
The frog has changed his yellow vest,
And in a russet coat is drest.
Though June, the air is cold, and still ;
The mellow blackbird's voice is shrill.
'Twill surely rain, I see with sorrow ;
Our jaunt must be put off to-morrow.

JENNER.

RETRANSLATION.

Through the glassy waters the fish rising to the air
  Catches with quick-glancing mouth the incautious flies.
In the shades of the past night many a glow-worm
  Was giving light to the valley, as the dew was falling.
The squalid toad in the meadow during the early twi-
    light   5
  Crawled and leaped alternately.
The sand obeys the commands of the revelling wind,
  And sweeps rapidly into eddies, a dusty cloud.
The frog has laid aside the saffron-coloured hues of his
    vest,
  And is hastening to assume, as is fitting, a tawny
    coat.   10
It is the month of June, but the air is dull and cold ;
  Nor does the voice of the blackbird now sound sweet,
    as before.
Ah! what heavy showers will follow such momentous
    signs :
  Alas ! we shall have-to-put-off our pleasant journey to-
    morrow.

HINTS.

2. "Quick-glancing," *micans.* Comp Virg. *Georg.* iii. 439.

3. "Glow-worm." As the native word, *cicindēla,* is inadmis-
sible from its quantity, the word *lampȳris (-ĭdis),* borrowed from the
Greek, may be used. It is found in Pliny.

4. "As the dew," etc., abl. absolute.

5. "Twilight." The Romans used two words, *dilūculum* for the
morning twilight, or dawn, and *crĕpusculum* (generally in the plural)
for the evening twilight, or dusk.

6. "Alternately," *alterna . . . vice.* Sometimes it is more convenient
to use the plural, *alternis . . . vicibus,* which is also good Latin.

8. "A dusty cloud," *pulverulenta* (adj), lit. "dusty."

10. "As is fitting," *ritē;* a word which has to be variously rendered to suit the context :—"in due form," "according to custom," etc.

11. "Month of June," *Junius mensis.* Our idiom prefers "the city *of* Rome," "the island *of* Cyprus," "the month *of* March," etc. "Is dull and cold," *friget languidus,* or *languet frigidus* Note this way of expressing a double predication in Latin.

12. "Blackbird." The word *merula,* for blackbird, is sanctioned by modern use, though not found in classical poetry. *Turdus* is found in the poets for thrush, but only as being a delicacy for the table. Comp Hor. *Sat.* i. 15. 41.

13. "Such momentous," *tot tantaque.*

14. "Shall have-to-put-off." Use the future perfect of *differo.*

EXERCISE LV.

THY witching look is like a two-edged sword,

   To pierce his heart by whom thou art surveyed ;

Thy rosy lips the precious balm afford

   To heal the wound thy keen-edged sword has made.

I am its victim ; I have felt the steel ;

   My heart now rankles with the smarting pain :

Give me thy lips the bitter wound to heal,—

   Thy lips to kiss, and I am whole again.

RETRANSLATION.

In the allurements of thy countenance there is an edge

   like a sharp sword,

  Wherewith to wound the heart of the beholder ;

Yet thy rosy mouth supplies precious medicines,
  To heal the piercing wounds of thy sword.
I am the victim of (thy) countenance; but lately (as) a
    victim, I felt the steel;   5
  A sharp pang torments my breast.
Give me (thy) lips, I pray, to heal the bitter wound;
  Give me to touch (thy) lips with mine; (and) I shall
    be whole.

HINTS.

1. "Allurements," *inlecebrae.*   "There is in," will be expressed by *inest,* at the end of line 2.

2. "Wherewith to wound," *quo* with 2d pers. pres. subj. of *lacero.* For this use of the subjunctive in a "final" clause, see the *Public School Latin Grammar,* § 208.   It will occur also in lines 4 and 7.

6. "Torments," *discrucial.*

8. "Whole," *sanus.*

EXERCISE LVI.

SHUN delays, they breed remorse;
  Take thy time, while time is lent thee;
Creeping snails have weakest force;
  Fly their fault, lest thou repent thee.
Good is best when soonest wrought,
  Lingering labour comes to nought.

Hoist up sail while gale doth last;
  Tide and wind stay no man's pleasure:
Seek not time when time is past;
  Sober speed is wisdom's leisure.
After-wit is dearly bought;
  Let thy forewit guide thy thought.

RETRANSLATION.

Away with delay! delay is harmful, if-procured by future
sorrow;

Seize the gifts that the present hour holds forth:

The sluggish worm scarce draws its own limbs along the
dust;

Avoid, whoever thou art, going after the manner of the
worm.

Those things above all are profitable, which profit
soonest;   5

The work which delay retards has no result.

Spread all thy sails to the breeze, as soon as the breeze has
invited thee;

Wave and breeze await no one's choice:

Seek not again the flying hour that is offered thee;

He who is wise pushes-on with circumspection the work
begun.   10

The wisdom that arises too late is dearly bought;

Let ready forethought point-out to thee the way.

HINTS.

1. "If-procured," pft. pass. participle.

3. "Along," sign of abl.

4. "After the manner of," *in exemplum*, following its genitive.

5. "Above all," *denique.* This word and *demum*, joined to
demonstratives, have a force like that of the Greek δή. Comp. Ov.
Am. iii. 4. 3, "ea denique casta est;" *Her.* xi. 91, "tunc demum
pectora plangi contigit."

7. "Sails," *sinus*, lit. "swelling," or "bellying" sails. "As soon
as," *simul*, with perf. subj.

9. "The flying hour that," *quae fugiens . . . horam.* Observe
the attraction to the relative clause of the epithet of "hour."

I

10. "With circumspection," "somewhat circumspectly," *cautior.*

11. "Dearly," *non . . . parvi.*   "Arises," *fit.*

12. "Ready forethought," *mens . . . quae praesto est provida.* Notice the allusion in the original to the προμήθεια and ἐπιμήθεια of the Greeks.

EXERCISE LVII.

(*The same continued.*)

TIME wears all his locks before ;
 Take thou hold upon his forehead ;
When he flies he turns no more,
 And behind displays a bare head.
Works adjourned have many stays ;
Long demurs breed new delays.

Seek thy salve while sore is green,
 Fester'd wounds ask deeper lancing ;
After-cures are seldom seen,
 Often sought, scarce ever chancing.
Time and place give best advice ;
Out of season, out of price.

SOUTHWELL.

RETRANSLATION.

See you not ?   Time wears in front all the locks that he
  has :
 Lest you should stumble, hold his forehead by main
  force :
When once he has fled-away, he turns his face no more ;
 Behind, his head is bare and bald.

Ofttimes labour flags, and grows slow of-itself by delaying; 5
   Ofttimes do deep designs breed fresh delays.
As soon as ever the sore appears, let a remedy be pre-
      pared;
   A neglected wound requires the help of the knife.
Rarely do medicines heal a fever, (now) strong by lapse
     of time;
   Often do men seek in vain things often to be sought. 10
A trustworthy adviser of action will be time, and (so will
     be) place;
   He who has foolishly neglected seasons, loses his means.

HINTS.

2. "By main force," *vique manuque.*

4. "Bald," *sine crine.*

5. "Grows slow," is retarded, *tardus fit.*

9. "Rarely," *rara*, to agree with the word for "medicines."

10. "Things often to be sought," *i.e.* which still elude the pur-
suit, *saepe petenda.*

11. "And so will be," expressed by merely repeating the epithet
fidus.

EXERCISE LVIII.

THE winds were laid, the air was still,
   The stars they shot along the sky;
The fox was howling on the hill,
   Whase distant echoing glens reply.

The stream adown its hazelly path
   Was rushing by the ruin'd wa's,
Hasting to join the sweeping Nith,
   Whase distant roaring swells and fa's.

The cauld blue north was streaming forth
Her lights, wi' hissing eerie din ;
Athort the lift they start and shift,
Like fortune's favours, tint as win.

RETRANSLATION.

The winds were now laid, and shooting through the silent void
The stars (were) seen to glitter through mid heaven.
The tawny fox fills the hill-side with dismal howlings ;
The wood echoes far off the reverberating sounds.
While the wave is wearing for itself a descending path
    through the hazel-groves,   5
It wastes-away the ruined walls with its headlong water,
While it hastens to blend with the sweeping Nīthus,
Which swells, and by turns the distant wave falls.
The blue North had darted its flames across the sky,
Phantoms, a hissing crowd, add their sounds.   10
It shoots and shifts its lights, like deceitful fortune,
    That gives and takes-away its gifts with alternate hand.

HINTS.

1. "Were laid." Comp. Virg. *Aen.* x. 103, "Tum Zephyri posuere."
"Shooting," *vibrata.*

3. "Tawny." Comp. Hor. *Car.* iii. 27. 3, "Rava decurrens lupa."

4. "Echoes," *dat*, with a suitable passive participle. In expressions of this kind the Latin is often too full to be adequately translated. Thus here, while *repercussos dat* would be sufficient, we really have *repercussos dat . . . icta.*

6. "Wastes away," lit. "eats away," *mordet.*

9. "North," *Arctos*, fem.

11. "It," *i.e. Arctos.* Hence begin with *Illa.* "Fortune," *fors*, to come in line 12, while the word for "gifts" will come in line 11. "Tint as win " = lost as they are won.

EXERCISE LIX.

(The same continued.)

By heedless chance I turn'd mine eyes,
　And, by the moonbeam, shook, to see
A stern and stalwart ghaist arise,
　Attired as minstrels wont to be.

Had I a statue been o' stane,
　His darin' look had daunted me ;
And on his bonnet graved was plain
　The sacred posie, Liberty.

And frae his harp sic strains did flow,
　Might rouse the slumbering dead to hear :
But oh ! it was a tale of woe,
　As ever met a Briton's ear.

He sang wi' joy his former day,
　He weeping wail'd his latter times ;
But what he said, it was nae play,
　I winna venture 't in my rhymes.

　　　　　　　　　　　　　　　BURNS.

RETRANSLATION.

By chance, as I was wandering through the rough-roads
　　beneath the moon's light,
　Visions, presented to my eyes, alarmed me.
Grim, and of more than human stature, and adorned with
　　a harp,
　A being seemed to be present in the midst of the way.

Now if I had been a block of Parian marble standing
    there,   5
  I could not but have feared the threats of his brow.
One might discern plain in the midst of his bonnet sacred
  Words, in which there was written : Love of Country.
You might think that his harp could rouse the shades
    from their graves,
  Such melting strains did it give back, when struck
    with the finger.   10
Yet the chords had a mournful ring, nor did any dirge
    before
  Sound more mournfully to an English ear.
Sadder (strains) succeed-to the joyful measures
  Which he exultingly poured forth about the glory of a
    former age ;
While he blames altered times, and pours forth serious 15
  Songs, that should hardly be weakened by my poor
    verses.

HINTS.

1. "As I was wandering," *pererrantem*, agreeing with *me* understood in the next line. "Rough roads," *salebras*.

3. "Of more than human stature," *humano major*.

4. "A being " *nescio quis*.

5. "Now if I had been . . . standing there," *Ast ego si starem.*

6. "I could not but," *non poteram . . . non.*

7. "Bonnet," *galerus.* Comp. Virg. *Aen.* vii. 688.

8. "In which there was written," *queis . . . scriptus inesset.*

10. "Such," *quos = quia tales.* This idiom is common in Greek,
as when *olovs* is found for ὅτι τοίους.

11. "Had a mournful ring," *Triste . . . crepuere.* The words
which follow are run together : "any before" end line 12, and "to an
ear " end line 11.

13, 14. These two lines will be in inverted order in the Latin ; 14

g the hexameter. The change is due to the sentence beginni
ι a relative clause.

ι6. "That should . . . be weakened," gerundive. Comp. H
n. iii. 3. 72, "magna modis tenuare parvis." "Poor verses." ι
diminutive.

EXERCISE LX.

Just Guardian of man's social bliss, for thee
    The paths of danger gladly would I tread ;
    For thee contented join the glorious dead,
Who nobly scorned a life that was not free.

But, worse than death, it pains my soul to see
    The lord of ruin, by wild uproar led,
    Hell's first-born, Anarchy, exalt his head,
And seize thy throne, and bid us bow the knee.

What though his iron sceptre, blood-imbrued,
    Crush half the nations with resistless might,
Never shall this firm spirit be subdued.
    In chains, in exile, still the chanted rite,
O Liberty, to thee shall be renewed :
    O still be sea-girt Albion thy delight.
                Poetry of the Anti-Jacobin.

Retranslation.

ɔu who guardest for man the joys of social life,
?or thee, goddess, I would suffer a thousand dangers

For thee I would even be joyfully added to the happy souls,
  In-whose-eyes a free death was preferable to heaven.
But when Licence, lover of ruin, sprung from Night,
      uproar   5
  Summoning, openly lifts her head to the stars,
And bids us be-slaves, wielding thy axes ;—
  When I watch this, it pains me more than death.
What though, dyeing Europe in blood with iron sceptre,
  She crush it with unconquerable force, and make it
      her own ?   10
Liberty ! to thee shall thy honours be duly proclaimed,
  Whether I be a captive or an exile.
There is here, there is (here) a soul which shall never be
    subdued.—
  May the land in the midst of the sea be to thee ever
    dear !

HINTS.

2. "Dangers." The syncopated form of *pericula* may be used. It must not be inferred that all nouns in *-ulum* can thus be shortened. For example, *pocla*, for *pocula*, is only found in Prudentius.

4. "In whose eyes," *queis*. "Free death," *liber Avernus ;* the thought being akin to Milton's "Better to reign in hell than serve in heaven."

5, 6. "Uproar summoning," *i.c.* "at the summons of uproar," *turba arcessente.*

7. "Wielding thy axes " Note the metaphor from consular state.

8. "It pains me," *dolet*, used absolutely, as in the beautiful epigram (Mart. i. 14) ending " sed quod tu facies, hoc mihi, Paete, dolet."

9. " Dyeing in blood," *cruentans*. For "iron sceptre," resort to the figure *hendiadys*, very common in Virgil, as *monstra . . . geminosque angues (Aen.* viii. 289), *arma . . . nodisque gravatum robur, pateris et auro.*

11. " Shall be proclaimed," *dicentur*.

12. " Exile," *fugitivus*.

EXERCISE LXI.

ON such an eve his palest beam he cast
When, Athens! here thy wisest look'd his last.
How watch'd thy better sons his farewell ray,
That closed their murder'd sage's latest day!
Not yet, not yet—Sol pauses on the hill,
The precious hour of parting lingers still;
But sad his light to agonising eyes,
And dark the mountain's once delightful dyes:
Gloom o'er the lovely land he seem'd to pour,
The land where Phœbus never frown'd before.
But ere he sunk below Cithæron's head,
The cup of woe was quaff'd, the spirit fled;
The soul of him that scorn'd to fear or fly,
Who lived and died as none can live or die.

BYRON.

RETRANSLATION.

In-such-wise too was Phœbus wan with western light,
  When the old-man perished in the learned city of Pallas.
With what solicitude by the faithful group was watched
  The last daylight, not to-return to their dear father!
But-not-yet on the lofty summit of the hill had paused   :
  The departing sun; nor yet had come the hour of (his)
    flight.
Yet gloomy and too-late it seemed to the eyes to linger,
  And that cloudless peak (was) hidden in shade.

You would have believed that with gloom was overspread
      the fair land
  On which the ray of Phœbus had always smiled before. 10
But before Cithæron reddened with the western light,
  The old-man had fearlessly drained the dread cup.
O resolute of soul, and to-be-bent by no danger !
  In-life thou wert alone ; in-death, alone.

Hints

3. "Solicitude," *pietas*. In what case will the agent be expressed
after a perfect passive, as *fuit . . . spectata ?*

5. "But-not-yet," *necdum.*

7. " Gloomy," *tristior.*

10. " On which," dative.

12. " Fearlessly." See note on xxix. 1.

13. "Of soul," *animi*, apparently a genitive, but really an instance
of the old locative case, ending in *i*, as all Greek datives. Comp.
victus animi, Virg. *Georg.* iv. 419 ; *amens animi, Aen.* iv. 370, etc.

EXERCISE LXII.

WHEN he who adores thee has left but the name
  Of his faults and his sorrows behind,
Oh ! say, wilt thou weep, when they blacken the fame
  Of a life that for thee was resign'd ?

Yes, weep ! for however my foes may condemn,
  Thy tears will efface their decree ;
For heaven can witness, though guilty to them,
  I have been but too faithful to thee.

With thee were the dreams of my earliest youth,
  Every thought of my reason was thine ;
In my last humble prayer to the Spirit above,
  Thy name shall be mingled with mine.

Oh ! blest are the lovers and friends who shall live
  The days of thy glory to see ;
But the next dearest blessing that Heaven can give
  Is the pride of thus dying for thee.

MOORE.

RETRANSLATION.

When, beyond titles of guilt and a harsh destiny,
  Thy constant lover has bequeathed thee nothing,
Wilt thou shed tears at least, when unjust revilings
  Crush the reputation of a life devoted to thee ?
Oh ! be mindful to weep: however the enemy may have
      defamed,   5
  Thy tears will blot-out his malicious word ;
For the enemy has-it-in-his-power to condemn : but I call
      heaven to witness,
  My only guilt in thy case is unbroken fidelity.
With thee I had of old my first dreams of love,
  And whatever I could revolve in mind (was) thine :   10
And when I a suppliant pay vows to God with my last
      prayer,
  One voice shall bear my name (and) one thine.
O thrice blessed companions and kindred by race,
  For whom the hour of thy glory may benignly smile ;
Yet dear is he to heaven, scarce inferior to them in his
      lot,   15
  Who has had the power and the will to die for thee.

HINTS.

1. "Titles," in the same sense as in St. John xix. 20, *titulos*.

2. "Thy constant," *tam benefidus*. Notice that in English we have often to leave untranslated a demonstrative in the Latin, when joined to possessive, demonstrative, or relative pronouns : *haec tanta, tuus tam fortis, quae tam iniqua*, etc.

3. "Shed tears," *dabis lacrimas*. Phrases with *dare* should be remembered. *Manus dare*, "to surrender ;" *terga dare*, "to fly ;" *verba dare alicui*, "to impose on a person." "When," etc. The words in this and the next line are run together. The word for "life" ends line 3, and that for "unjust" comes in line 4.

7. "Heaven," *sidera*, lit. "the stars."

8. "In thy case," *in te*.

14. "Benignly," *alma*.

15. "Inferior," *secundus*.

16. "Has had the power," *potuit*. Express in the same way, "has had the will."

EXERCISE LXIII.

SHE is far from the land where her young hero sleeps,
    And lovers are round her sighing ;
But coldly she turns from their gaze, and weeps,
    For her heart in his grave is lying.

She sings the wild song of her dear native plains,
    Every note which he loved, awaking :
Ah ! little they think, who delight in her strains,
    How the heart of the minstrel is breaking.

He had lived for his love, for his country he died ;
    They were all that to life had entwined him ;
Nor soon shall the tears of his country be dried,
    Nor long will his love stay behind him.

Oh ! make her a grave where the sunbeams rest
   When they promise a glorious morrow ;
They'll shine o'er her sleep like a smile from the west,
   From her own loved island of sorrow.

MOORE.

RETRANSLATION.

She stands far from the land where thou, famous youth,
   dost sleep ;
Thy maiden stands, worshipped by anxious suitors ;
But coldly she turns-away her tearful eyes, and thither
   Flees in thought (*lit.* mind), where the turf covers his
   dear head.
Soon from her native harp she hastily draws-forth what-
   ever   5
Strains her lover had once been glad to hear :
Nor do the groups drinking-in (the music) with eager ear
   perceive
That she who sings is slowly dying with failing heart.
For his country he fell, who had lived all for love :
   No other motive was there, why he should survive.   10
And-not with short-lived grief of his country will the
   hero be mourned ;
And soon will the maiden follow her youthful lover.
Lay ye (her), where the light of the setting sun reminds
   (us)
   How great is-likely-to-be the glory of the returning
   god :
(Her) island will seem to have smiled on her across the
   waves,   15
   An island made dearer by its own troubles.

HINTS.

3. "Coldly." See note on xxix. 1. On the same principle translate "had been glad to hear," in line 6.

5. End with *si quae*, = εἴ τινα.

6. *Amans*, for "lover," being really a noun, may end the line.

8. Begin with the relative.

10. "No other," etc. lit. "nothing else of cause."—In what mood
will the following verb be, after *cur*, and why?

11. "And . . . not," *nec.*

12. "And soon," etc. Turn by *nec mora . . . erit*, inserting a
clause with *quin* and the subjunctive.

14. "Is likely to be," *sit . . . futura.* Why is the verb in the
subjunctive mood?

EXERCISE LXIV.

THY voice is heard thro' rolling drums,
    That beat to battle where he stands;
Thy face across his fancy comes,
    And gives the battle to his hands.
A moment, while the trumpets blow,
    He sees his brood about thy knee;
The next, like fire, he meets the foe,
    And strikes him dead for thine and thee.

                                    TENNYSON.

RETRANSLATION.

When the drums thunder with beating, when thy soldier
    in arms
  Stands, about-to-go to the uncertain work of Mars,
He sees thee, and, rejoicing in the form seen, the fight
  In sure hope claims for his own hands.

While the clarions and the blown trumpets are braying,　5
　　He beholds his children, dear pledges, on thy knees.
At once, like lightning, he rushes headlong ; he strikes the
　　　foeman
　　For thee ; for thy children lo ! he lays him low.

HINTS.

1. " Thunder," *reboant.*　" Thy " will come in the second line.

3. " Rejoicing," perf. partic. of *gaudeo.*

4. " For his own," *ipse suis.*　See note on **xxv.** 12.

6. " Children," *natos,* to end line 5.

7. " Like lightning," *flamma velut.*　" Strikes," *occupat ;* lit.
" anticipates in striking."

EXERCISE LXV.

" A WEARY lot is thine, fair maid,
　　A weary lot is thine !
　To pull the thorn thy brow to braid,
　　And press the rue for wine.
　A lightsome eye, a soldier's mien,
　　A feather of the blue,
　A doublet of the Lincoln green—
　　No more of me you knew,
　　　　　My love !
　No more of me you knew.

" This morn is merry June, I trow ;
　　The rose is budding fain ;
　But she shall bloom in winter snow
　　Ere we two meet again."

He turned his charger as he spake
Upon the river shore ;
He gave his bridle reins a shake,
Said, "Adieu for evermore,
My love !
And adieu for evermore !"

SCOTT.

RETRANSLATION.

"Thou longest-for a thankless lot, fairest Delia ;
Thou wilt lament prolonged weariness of a forsaken
couch ;
In that thou desirest to bind thy brow with the painful
thorn,
And to ask the rue for gifts of cheerless wine.
That I had merry eyes, the keen look of a soldier,   5
(And) that the plume of my helmet was azure, thou
didst know ;
Thou didst know that I was clad in the green mantle of
a hunter :
Beyond this, Delia, thy love knew nothing.
Lo ! the month of June is smiling, sweetest of the year,
And the roses have gladly unfolded their buds.   10
But they will dare to trust the winter sky, before
That favouring time restores thee to me, me to thee."
Thus he speaks, and with averted looks at the same time,
and not saying more,
He turned his steed back on the river's bank ;
He turned his steed ; and again, shaking the reins, "Fare-
well,"   15
He said, "for ever, beloved Delia, farewell ! "

HINTS.

1. "Longest for," *expetis*.

3. "In that," etc., causal subjunctive, *quae . . . cupias*.

4. "Ask for " Remember that verbs of asking govern two accusatives.

5. "That I had, *esse . . . mihi*.

7. "That I was clad," *indutum*. In what case will the word expressing the covering be ?

8. "Beyond this," *haec praeter*.

11, 12. "Before that." *Priusquam* and *antequam* may be used with their separate parts, if necessary, in different lines. "Favouring time," *fausta dies*.

13. "With averted looks," *aversus*.

14. "River's," expressed by the adjective in agreement.

EXERCISE LXVI.

AND ne'er did Grecian chisel trace
A Nymph, a Naiad, or a Grace,
Of finer form or lovelier face.
What though the sun, with ardent frown,
Had slightly tinged her cheek with brown ;—
The sportive toil which, short and light,
Had dyed her glowing hue so bright,
Served too in hastier swell to show
Short glimpses of a breast of snow.
What though no rule of courtly grace
To measured mood had trained her pace ;—
A foot more light, a step more true,
Ne'er from the heath-flower dash'd the dew :
E'en the slight hare-bell raised its head,
Elastic, from her airy tread.
SCOTT.

K

RETRANSLATION.

No Naiad or Grace from Phidias' hand
 Was nobler in form, more beautiful in face.
Although the rude sun, looking-down from mid Olympus,
 Had not suffered her cheeks to be untouched by (his) fire,
Yet the sport, brief as it was, and of easy toil,   5
 Whence the unaccustomed flush now came into her
  countenance,
Was the cause of your being able to see
 How snowy a bosom the drapery more and more quickly
  moved did cover.
What though no acquaintance with royal hall had taught
  (her)
 To pace with measured movement,   10
No (footstep) lighter or surer than that footstep
 Would brush the dew from the grassy glebe.
Nay even the green heather rises-again, as she treads,
 Not injured by a step too heavily pressed upon it.

HINTS.

1. "From," use *a*, with the ablative of the adjective formed from Phidias, *Phidiacus*. The first three lines of the original make two in Latin.

3. "Rude," *asper*. Note how the sense is strengthened by the insertion of a phrase to express "midday." As *medius Olympus* conveys this idea, so *devexus Olympus* would be a phrase for evening.

5. "As it was," *ille quidem*. *Ille quidem* sometimes expresses what we convey by emphasising a spoken word, as "no fool *he* !" "non insipiens ille quidem."

7. "Of your being able," *ut . . . posses*.

8. "Drapery," *carbasa*, neut. pl. The words for "more and more quickly," *citius . . . citiusque*, come in the previous line.

9. "Acquaintance with royal hall," *aulae . . . regius usus*.

10. " To pace," *ferre referre pedem.* To express a *majestic* gait you would imitate Virgil's " incedit regina."

12. " Glebe," *humus.*

14. " Too heavily," *altius.* For the description, compare what is said of Camilla, Virg. *Aen.* vii. 808 *sqq.*

EXERCISE LXVII.

THE hall was clear'd ; the stranger's bed
Was there of mountain heather spread,
Where oft a hundred guests had lain,
And dream'd their forest sports again.
But vainly did the heath-flower shed
Its moorland fragrance round his head :
Not Ellen's spell had lull'd to rest
The fever of his troubled breast.
In broken dreams the image rose
Of varied perils, pains, and woes :
His steed now flounders in the brake,
Now sinks his barge upon the lake ;
Now, leader of a broken host,
His standard falls, his honour's lost.

RETRANSLATION.

The hall is empty and forsaken ; the stranger lies in the
    empty hall ;
  The heather spreads a mountain couch for his head ;
Many a throng of-hunters there wooed slumber,
  Seeming in dreams to be again transfixing the quarry.
Now however the heather wafts mountain odours to no
    purpose,   5
  Which sprinkles the brows of the wearied man.

The charms of thy song, Dëïdămĭă,
  Were able to no purpose to heal the furies of his breast.
Varied perils (seemed) to rise and assume doubtful forms,
  And sorrows seemed (to rise) and uneasy pain.   10
And one-while his charger (seemed) to be stumbling
        along the rugged brakes,
  Now his bark to perish overwhelmed in the midst of
        the lake.
And again, as a leader, he is vainly rallying his broken
        squares,
  And falling standards betoken honour lost.

HINTS.

  1. "Is empty and forsaken," *relicta vacat*.   Comp. Ex. xxv. 8.
  3. "Of hunters," *venatrix*, adj.
  4. "Quarry," *feras*.
  5. "Heather," to come in line 6.
  7, 8. Reverse the order of these two lines in the Latin.
  9. "Rise and assume," *surgere in*, with acc.
  11. "Brakes," *salebras*, lit. "rugged roads." Comp. Ex. lix. 1.
  13. "Is rallying," *ciet ore*.
  14. "Betoken," *monent*.

EXERCISE LXVIII.

(*The same continued.*)

THEN—from my couch may heavenly might
Chase that worst phantom of the night!
Again returned the scenes of youth,
Of confident, undoubting truth;
Again his soul he interchanged
With friends whose hearts were long estranged.

> They come, in dim procession led,
> The cold, the faithless, and the dead ;
> As warm each hand, each brow as gay,
> As if they parted yesterday :
> And doubt distracts him at the view :—
> O were his senses false or true ?
>
> SCOTT.

RETRANSLATION.

And by turns—such dread visions of the night far hence
　From my chamber may propitious deities turn away !
By turns comes back again the hour of early youth,
　Truthful ingenuousness and fairer faith.
Again is joined of former friendship the close　　　　　　5
　Link, alas ! dissevered in length of time.
Lo there comes slow-moving in dim line a faithless band,
　And (those) whom Libitina has carried-off with cold
　　hand.
Each one has a warm right hand , each has such grace of
　　brow,
　You would believe that (only) yesterday had parted
　　them.　　　　　　10
As he sees it, the uncertain phantom distracts him in a
　　twofold way :
　Is he deceived ? or can sense be disclosing what-is-true ?

HINTS.

1. "Visions," *insomnia.*

3. "By turns : " repeat the *Inque vices* of line 1.

7. "Slow-moving," *tractim* (adv.)　"Band," *ordo.*

9. "Each one has," etc., lit., "the right-hand is warm for each," *cuivis*, = "any one you please."

11. "As," etc.　Use the animated form of expression, *Ut videt, ut, etc.*　See **xxix.** 5.　"Phantom," *imago.*

EXERCISE LXIX.

You meaner beauties of the night,
 That poorly satisfy our eyes
More by your number than your light,
 You common people of the skies ;
 What are you, when the sun shall rise ?

You curious chanters of the wood,
 That warble forth dame Nature's lays,
Thinking your voices understood
 By your weak accents ; what's your praise,
 When Philomel her voice shall raise ?

You violets that first appear
 By your pure purple mantles known,
Like the proud virgins of the year,
 As if the spring were all your own ;
 What are you, when the rose is blown ?

So when my mistress shall be seen
 In form and beauty of her mind,
By virtue first, then choice, a Queen,
 Tell me, if she were not design'd
 Th' eclipse and glory of her kind ?

WOTTON.

RETRANSLATION.

Plebeian company of stars, ignoble herd,
 An inferior throng, that crowd the pathway of night,

You that hold our gaze more by number than by light,—
    Have you any honour when risen day is shining ?
O race, taught woodland sounds, cultivators of melodies, 5
    Which you pour forth by Nature's help, unskilled in
        art,
Striving to express your feelings in slender strain,—
    Have you any honour when the nightingale sings ?
You violets that first lead-on the entire year,
    That deem the days of-spring to be moving-on for
        you,   10
Known by your purple covering and chaste disdain,—
    Have you any honour when the rose comes on ?
So when at length my queen appears in honour,
    (She) whom virtue first has raised, then promotion,
Surpassing in mind and beauty :—must it not be owned 15
    That she alone is the glory of the human name ?

HINTS.

2. "Inferior," *minor*. The following relative, after a noun of multitude, may be in the plural. Note also that the first four lines of every stanza have to be condensed into three, and mark the various devices by which this is done.

4. "Have you any . . . " *ecquis (est) vobis.*

5. "Taught." If "docui te artes" is "I taught you arts," what will "you were taught arts" be ? "Cultivators of," *studiosa*, with genitive.

9. "Lead on," *duco.*

10. "To be moving on," *ire.*

14. "Promotion," *vices*, lit. a *succeeding* to honour.

EXERCISE LXX.

THERE is one tree which now I call to minde,
Doth beare these verses carued in his rinde :
" When Geraldine shall sit in thy faire shade,
Fanne her sweet tresses with perfumed aire,
Let thy large boughes a canopie be made,
To keep the sunne from gazing on my faire,
And when thy spredding branched arms be suncke,
And thou no sap nor pith shalt more retaine,
Eu'n from the dust of thy unweldy truncke,
I will renue thee Phœnix-like againe,
And from thy dry decayed root will bring
A new-borne stem, another Aeson's spring."

DRAYTON.

RETRANSLATION.

An oak-tree there is, I remember, which, marked with my
knife,
  Has this ditty on its rugged bark :
" Oak-tree, as often as Lalage reposes in (thy) shade, let
  A sweet breeze fan her perfumed locks ;
And let thy leafy branches spread thick canopies,   5
  That Phœbus may not first reach the face of my Lalage.
So for thy deserts will I, when thy branching vigour grows
  old,
  The sap now failing thy veins,
Cause that, from the ashes of (thy) huge trunk, thy form
  surviving
  Shall rise again, like the Phœnix.   10

So shall thy life be renewed, like old Aeson,
　And there shall be fresh beauty of verdure from thy
　　decayed stock.

HINTS.

1. "Oak-tree," *aesculus* (winter-oak). Notice the substitution of a particular term for a general. "Marked," in agreement with "ditty" in the next line. "Knife," *falx.*

2. "Ditty," *carmen.*

3. "Let," *fac*, followed by the subj.

5. "Canopies," *umbracula.*

6. "First reach," *occupet.*

7. "Branching vigour," *vis ramosa.*

9. "Will cause that," *faciam*, to come in line 10, followed by subj.

10. "Like the Phœnix," lit. "after the manner of the Panchæan (*i.e.* Arabian) bird." Comp. Ov. *Met.* x. 478.

11. "Like," *instar*, with gen. For Aeson (gen. Aesŏnis), comp. Ov. *Met.* vii. 287 *sqq.*

12. Lit. "And a fresh honour shall be green from," etc. "Stock," *stirps.*

EXERCISE LXXI.

LYKE as a ship, that through the ocean wyde
　By conduct of some star doth make her way,
When as a storm hath dimm'd her trusty guyde,
　Out of her course doth wander far astray ;
　　So I, whose star, that wont with her bright ray
Me to direct, with cloudes is overcast,
　Do wander now, in darkness and dismay,
Through hidden perils round about me plac'd ;

Yet hope I well that, when the storm is past,
  My Helice, the load-star of my lyfe,
Will shine again, and look on me at last
  With lovely light to clear my cloudy grief.
Till then I wander carefull, comfortlesse,
In secret sorrow and sad pensiveness.

SPENSER.

RETRANSLATION.

As a ship that, through the distant waters of ocean,
  A star pointing-out the way, directs its course,
If a dangerous storm has dimmed the friendly ray,
  Is driven from her course, roaming at her own will ;
So I, whose star, long with steady light me   5
  To lead accustomed, thick clouds overwhelm,
Disturbed by portents, dismayed by darkness, am wander-
      ing
  Through misfortunes lying-in-wait for my fortunes.
Yet a sustaining hope lurks in my mind, that, when the
      storm is abated,
  The star's ray will shine with familiar flame.   10
Thou, Helice, sole guide of my life, wilt propitiously
  Dispel the darkness and restore the day.
Meanwhile, keeping sorrow beneath silent breast,
  Restless, helpless, I wander thus without light.

HINTS.

1. "As," *qualiter*.
8. "Dangerous," *mala*.
4. "At her own will," *sponte . . . sua*.
5. "Whose," *cui*.
9. "Lurks in my mind," *subest mihi*.

11. "Helice." Comp. Lucan ii. 237, "Parrhasis obliquos Helic cum verteret axes." Helice was a name for the constellation of Urs Major. Observe the device by which the sense is kept from runnin on from the 10th to the 11th line, as in the English.

EXERCISE LXXII.

THE weary mariner so fast not flies
   An howling tempest, harbour to obtain,
Nor shepherd hastes, when frays of wolves arise,
   So fast to fold, to save his bleating team,
As I, wing'd with contempt and just disdain,
   Now fly the world, and what it most doth prize,
And sanctuary seek, free to remain
   From wounds of abject time and envy's eyes.
Once did this world to me seem sweet and fair,
   While senses light mind's prospective kept blind.
Now, like imagin'd landscape in the air,
   And weeping rainbows, her best joys I find.
Or, if aught here is had that praise should have,
It is an obscure and a silent grave.

                    DRUMMOND.

RETRANSLATION.

Not more quickly does the sailor shun the rising storm,
   If he be able to reach a safe harbour,
Nor flies the shepherd, on hearing alarm of wolves
   More swiftly, to guard his sheep penned-up,
Than my mind, roused with anger and just disdain,
   Now flees-from the people and what pleased the people,
And seeks a sacred refuge, where I may be able to live
   Safe from envy and from my times.

Formerly, while light senses were inhabiting (my) blind
    breast,

  Life used-to-seem beautiful and pleasing to me.   10

Now I complain that the greatest things it offers have
    melted away, like mountain-tops,

  In air deceiving, or else the rainbow's gleam.

Or, if there still remains something to be praised, there
    remains

  To-be-wished-for the little grave of an obscure pyre.

HINTS.

1. "Sailor," to begin line 2.

2. "A safe harbour." Imitate Virgil's "opaca locorum," "strata viarum."

5. "And just," turn by a double negative, "and not unjust," remembering that "and not" is expressed by *nec*.

11. "The greatest things it offers." The antecedent *maxima* is drawn by attraction into the relative clause. So often with *solus*, *multus*, *plurimus*, etc. Comp. *Aen.* xi. 352, "donis istis, quae plurima mitti . . . jubes." "Mountain-tops," *arces*. Comp *Aen* vii. 696.

14. "Grave," *busta*.

EXERCISE LXXIII.

CALL it not vain! They do not err,
  Who say that, when the poet dies,
Mute Nature mourns her worshipper,
  And celebrates his obsequies:
Who say tall cliff and cavern lone
For the departed bard make moan ,
That mountains weep in crystal rill,
That flowers in tears of balm distil;

Through his loved grove that breezes sigh,
And oaks in deeper groan reply ;
And rivers teach their rushing wave
To murmur dirges round his grave.

RETRANSLATION.

Think it not something vain ; for neither does a flitting
    fancy mock (those)
Who affirm that all things complain when a bard dies ;
To whom the whole landscape seems in-silence
    To be solemnizing obsequies for its own worshipper.
In sooth, as they tell, when the sweet poet dies,   5
    The lofty hills and hollow rocks moan :
The mountain heights far-and-wide shed tears in crystal
    rills ;
    The wood, as if weeping, distils with the perfume of
    flowers ;
The sighs of the Zephyr float-over the groves that he loved,
    While oaks in deeper tones re-echo the sounds ;   10
And rivers, as they feign, teach their rushing waves to
    grow-gentle,
    And to raise a sorrowful murmur at his tomb.

HINTS.

1. "Not something," *ne quid.* "Flitting," *vaga.*

2. "When," etc., use the ablative absolute. So in line 5.

3. "Landscape," *rerum species.* Observe that the Romans had no direct word for either "landscape," "scenery," or "picturesque." Virgil's "silvis *scena* coruscis," and Horace's "Thessala Tempe" (for a beautiful valley) are phrases that may be useful.

6. "Lofty," *aerii.* Comp. Virg. *Aen.* iii. 291.

11. "Teach," *docent,* to come at the end of line 12.

EXERCISE LXXIV.

(The same continued).

NOT that, in sooth, o'er mortal urn
These things inanimate can mourn ;
But that the stream, the wood, the gale,
Is vocal with the plaintive wail
Of those who, else forgotten long,
Lived in the poet's faithful song,
And, with the poet's parting breath,
Whose memory feels a second death.
The maid's pale shade, who wails her lot
That love, true love, should be forgot,
From rose and hawthorn shakes the tear
Upon the gentle minstrel's bier.

RETRANSLATION.

Not that by mortal urns, if we confess the truth,
  Things that are themselves devoid of souls can mourn ;
Yet undoubtedly the streams, and woods, and the tearful
    breeze
  Will be charged with the re-echoing voice of the mourner,
For whomsoever, otherwise destined to meet-with dull
    forgetfulness,   5
  His honour has continued undying in the poet's faithful
    song :
Soon as the poet departs, there departs for him the time of
    memory,
  And a second death to-be-undergone awaits (him) lifeless.

Am I mistaken, or does the shade of the virgin who bewails
    The lot of obscure love, bring dewy roses,   10
And will she mindfully shake-off from white thorns a shower
    Upon the peaceful earth, where the bard reposes ?

HINTS.

1. "The truth," *vera* (neut. pl.)

2. "That are devoid," *i.e.* "such as are devoid," generalizing, *quae careant* (*subj.*) So the verb for "can," *queant*, will be in the subjunctive after *non quia*, because a hypothetical proposition is denied. The verb in line 4, stating the simple fact, will of course be in the indicative.

4. "Charged," *crebra.* The exact idea of the word is that it will come "thick and fast," the opposite of *rarus.*

5. "For whomsoever," *cui . . . cumque* (by tmesis).

6. "The poet's," *vatis*, to come at the end of line 5. "Has continued," *steterit.* Why subjunctive ?

7. "Soon as," *ut . . . ut;* comp. note on xxix. 5. "Time of memory," *i.e.* in which he is kept in memory, *memorabilis aetas.*

9. "Am I mistaken, or," etc., *Fallor, an, etc.* Observe how this turn gives more vividness, and also takes off the slight abruptness that there would be in closely rendering "The maid's pale shade," etc.

10. "Brings," *affert.*

EXERCISE LXXV.

(*The same continued.*)

THE phantom knight, his glory fled,
Mourns o'er the field he heap'd with dead ;
Mounts the wild blast that sweeps amain,
And shrieks along the battle plain.

The chief, whose antique crownlet long
Still sparkled in the feudal song,
Now, from the mountain's misty throne,
Sees, in the thanedom once his own,
His ashes undistinguish'd lie,
His place, his power, his memory die.
His groans the lonely caverns fill,
His tears of rage impel the rill.
All mourn the minstrel's harp unstrung,
Their name unknown, their praise unsung.

SCOTT.

RETRANSLATION.

The semblance of the knight, with fallen splendour, moves
sighing
Over the funeral-mounds now heaped-up by his right hand.
Or else is borne on the sweeping blasts, and wailing roams
Where he had consigned to death a thousand fallen
warriors.
The chieftain too, for whom through the subservient harp
his ancient coronet 5
Still glittered, scarce dimmed by long lapse of time,
Now marks, how changed! from the misty seat of the hills,
The lands which his long lineage gave him.
Lo! the hapless one feels that his ashes lie without honour :
His name, his power, his titles, and local reverence, are
no more. 10
When he sees (it), how he redoubles his groans through
the forsaken caves,
How he impels the swollen waters of the river with his
tears !

Each-one mourns his praises silent, his name unhonoured,
    And (mourns) that the chords of the minstrel harp are
        silent and unstrung.

HINTS.

1. "Moves," *it*, to begin the line.

4. "A thousand fallen warriors," *funera mille virum.* The successive meanings of *funus* should be remembered : (1) a funeral, (2) a corpse, (3) death or destruction.

5. "Coronet." It seems natural to use *corona*, or *corolla ;* but in strictness these only mean "garland." A king's crown or headdress was *diadema.*

6. "Dimmed," "tarnished," *temerata ;* "lapse of time," *mora.*

7. "Changed," acc. plural, referring to "lands."

8. "Lineage," comp. Juv. *Sat.* viii. 1, "*Stemmata* quid faciunt ? quid prodest, Pontice, *longo* | sanguine censeri," etc.

9. "The hapless one feels that they lie," *jacent misero.* The use of the dative of the indirect object conveys this meaning. "Turnus's spirits rose," "Turni crevere animi." "Turnus felt his spirits rise," "Turno crevere animi."

10. "Local reverence," *relligio loci.* "Are no more," *fuere*, to end line 9. For the word, comp. Virg. "*fuit* Ilium, et ingens | gloria Teucrorum."

11. "When" . . . "how," *ut* . . . *ut.*

14. "Are silent and unstrung." See note above on **XXV.** 8.

EXERCISE LXXVI.

HYMN TO THE SEASONS.

WHEN spring unlocks the flowers,
    To paint the laughing soil,
When summer's balmy showers
    Refresh the mower's toil,

L

When winter binds in frosty chains
  The fallow and the flood ;
In God the earth rejoiceth still,
  And owns its Maker good.

The birds that wake the morning,
  And those that love the shade,
The winds that sweep the mountain,
  Or lull the drowsy glade,
The sun that from his amber bower
  Rejoiceth on his way,
The moon, the stars, their Maker's name
  In silent pomp display.

HEBER.

RETRANSLATION.

Whether gladsome spring unlocks the bright flowers,
  And paints with fresh grass the laughing ground,
Or the balmy shower, falling from summer cloud,
  Refreshes the bodies of the reapers overcome by the
    heat,
Or icy winter binds on-every-side the sluggish fields,   *
  And curbs the running waters with its hard fetter ;
The earth bears-witness-to God, and joyfully through all
    hours
  Proclaims that the Author of the universe is good.

The birds that in the morning salute the day with cheer-
    ful voice,
  And (those) which the shade of quiet evening rather
    delights,   1C

The winds that now sweep the mountains with tearing blast,
  The gentler breeze that now lulls the drowsy wood,
The sun that goes forth most beautiful from his saffron-
      coloured bower,
  Rejoicing to enter the way of his celestial path,
And the moon, and the stars shining in silent procession,—15
  All created things acknowledge a divine hand.

HINTS.

1. "Gladsome," *laetabile.*   "Bright :" comp. Virg. "*purpureos*que
jacit flores."

3. "Balmy," *tener.*

6. "Curbs," *fraenat.*   "Running," *celeres.*

8. "Universe," *res* (pl.) The adj. for "good," being emphatic,
is allowed to end this line.

11. "Tearing," *rapidus.*   "Blast," *turbine.*

12. "Drowsy," *iners.*

13. "Saffron-coloured," *croceus.*

14. "Path," *trames, -itis.*

15. "Procession," *pompa.*

EXERCISE LXXVII.

Sweet bird, that sing'st away the early hours,
      Of winters, past or coming, void of care,
      Well pleased with delights that present are,
Fair seasons, budding spray, sweet-smelling flowers ;
To rocks, to springs, to rills, from leafy bowers
      Thou thy Creator's goodness dost declare,
      And what dear gifts to thee he did not spare,
A stain to human sense, in sin that lowers.

What soul can be so sick, which by thy songs
  (Attired in sweetness) sweetly is not driven
Quite to forget earth's turmoils, spites and wrongs,
  And lift a reverent eye and thought to heaven !
Sweet artless songster, thou my mind dost raise
To airs of spheres, yea, and to Angels' lays.

DRUMMOND.

RETRANSLATION.

Careless of winter past, careless of (winter) to come,
  Sweet bird, thou wearest away the spring time with song:
In truth, present joys please thee enough,—flowers
  Bright, cloudless spring, and verdant sprays.
How great (is) the goodness of the Supreme Father, what
      gifts propitiously   5
  He bestows upon thee with no sparing hand,
Thou utterest in the midst of the grove to rocks and
      fountains,
  While our sin weighs us down and forbids to speak.
For who (is) so weary of the world, as not to be touched
      by thy
  Songs, voiced in honeyed strains ;   10
As not to be compelled to let go human cares,
  And with pure mind and eyes to seek-after heaven !
While thou, artless one, makest thy music, I seem to hear
  The harmony of the spheres and the choirs of the
      celestials.

HINTS.

2. "Sweet bird," *flos avium.*

4. "Bright," *purpurei.* See note on lxxvi. 1.

5. "Propitiously," *praesens.*

8. Observe how the sense of this line in the original is made clearer.
The grateful song of the bird serves as a reflection on "human sense"

(the ungrateful feelings of man) "lowering in sin," like the "curvae in terras animae" of Persius.

9. "The world," *rerum.* "As not to be touched by," *quem non* (*tangunt* or *tangant ?*) See the *Public School Latin Grammar* (1883), p. 456, and note on lxxiv. 2.

10. "Voiced," *articulata.*

11. "As not," etc. Take the active turn, as in ver. 9, with the same mood.

13. "Artless one," *arte carens.* "I seem," to come in line 14, while "of the spheres" ends line 13.

EXERCISE LXXVIII.

Two summer morns alike may break,
And bid the wood's sweet anthems wake :
And one shall mark its sun descend
Unclouded to his glorious end ;
And one shall see the whirlwind rise,
And storm and gloom enshroud its skies.

Two summer larks alike may spring,
At daybreak, on their upward wing :
And this, at eve, shall carol loud
Beneath her canopy of cloud ;
And that, before the west is grey,
Shall flutter as the fowler's prey.

RETRANSLATION.

It may be that two days sprung alike from summer source,
    Rouse harmony through all the grove :

This one shall behold the sun undimmed, speeding on
> without a cloud,
Go straight to the goal of his ruddy way.
That one (shall see) the north-wind and the violence of
> the tempest increase.   5
And the sky soon overspread with storm and blackness.
It may be that, at early morn, larks, the nurslings of
> summer,
Start-on their airy flight, a gladsome pair :
The one, at eventide, shall tunefully utter a clear song,
> Where the shade of a hanging cloud screens it as it
> flutters ;   10
The other, ere the sun has darkened the western world,
> Will quiver, the fowler's prey, in-death upon the ground.

HINTS.

1. "It may be that," *est ut,* with subjunctive.

3. "Without a cloud," lit. "without a stain."   Comp. Prop. iv. 8. 20, "famae non sine labe meae."

4. "Go." The verb here, as in the next two lines, will be in the infinitive.

7. "Nurslings," *soboles.*—Note the turn by which the stiff formality of recurring expressions is avoided ; as also in the use of *par genuale,* in apposition to *alaudae,* to express "two."

9. "The one," "the other." As a pair of birds is spoken of, *hic* and *haec* may be properly used, which will also serve to vary the phrase. For two summer mornings, not rising together, *hic* and *ille* were appropriate. In like manner, *altera-alterius* will suit lines 15 and 17.

10. "As-it-flutters," *tremulum.* Compare, for the subject, Virg. *Aen.* v. 515-8.

11. "Has darkened," *i.e.* by its departure. Comp. Virg. *Aen.* iii. 508, "Sol ruit interea et montes umbrantur opaci ;" and, for the word to be used, Ovid's "*Fuscabat*que diem custos Erymanthidos ursae."

12. "In death," *emoriens.*

EXERCISE LXXIX.

(*The same continued.*)

Two rosebuds shall alike be seen
To burst their shrine of emerald green :
And one shall shed its life-long breath
In sweetness, and be sweet in death ;
And one, ere yet 'tis fully burst,
With mildew and with blight be curst.
And so these twain—this hour shall view
Which is the feigned and which the true.

NEALE.

RETRANSLATION.

Perchance, too, it may have happened to twin roses
    To burst open together the shrine of their green calyx :
The one breathes its sighs of-sweetness through all its life,
    Soon to enter in-sweetness on the way of death.
The bud of the other, while it has not yet grown and
        come to maturity,   5
    Mildew or blackening blight devours in unproductive-
        ness.
Even so the passing hour will show, of these daughters,
    Which shall be called faithful, which false.

HINTS.

1, 2. The words in these two lines are blended together. Use
penetrale for "shrine" in 1, and *vi reserdsse* for "to burst open" in 2.

3. "Of-sweetness," *suavia*, to come in verse 4   "In-sweetness"
will be rendered by the same adjective.

5. "Grown and come to maturity." Use *aucta* with perf. subj. of *adolesco.*

6. "In unproductiveness," *sterilem.*

7, 8. These lines are blended, like 1 and 2. "Will show" is to be rendered by *indicio . . . dabit*, to begin and end line 8. "Which" (of two) is *utra*. For "to be called" *audire* may be used, as in Horace's "Matutine pater, seu Jane libentius audis."

EXERCISE LXXX.

WHAT doth it serve to see the sun's bright face,
    And skies enamell'd with the Indian gold,
    Or the bright moon in car of silver roll'd,
And all the glory of that starry place ?
    What doth it serve earth's beauty to behold,
The mountain's pride, the meadow's flowery grace,
    The stately comeliness of forests old,
The sport of floods which would the earth embrace ?
    What doth it serve to hear the sylvans' songs,
The cheerful thrush, the nightingale's sad strains,
    Which in dark shades seems to deplore my wrongs ?
For what doth serve all that this world contains,
    Since one, for whom those once to me were dear,
    Can now no longer share them with me here ?

RETRANSLATION.

What pleasure is it to gaze-on the bright face of Phœbus, or
    The variegated temples of the sky that resemble Indian
        gold ?
What pleasure is Cynthia rolling in silvery car,
    Or the manifold glories of the starry region ?

Is it worth while to behold how fair the earth is,   5
   What beauty the meadows have, what glory the heights?
With what stateliness the aged forests wave,
   Or how the sportive billow seeks to embrace the earth?
What boots it me to hear the hum of the denizens-of-the-
      woods,
   The clear notes of the blackbird, the plaint of the night-
      ingale?   10
Mourns she indeed or seems to mourn-for me in dark
      shades?
   Nought does she, nought does anything profit that lives
      in the world.
For the sweet one has gone, along with whom all things
      were sweet to me ;
   The sharer of my joy, not to-return.

HINTS.

  2. "Indian," *Indum*, to come at the end of line 1.
  3. "Silvery," *argenteo*, scanned as a trisyllable, by synizesis.
  4. "Manifold," *multiplicata*.
  6. "What." *Quale* may be used in one clause, *quanta* in the other.
  7. "Wave," *coruscent ;* comp. Juv. *Sat.* iii. 264.
  10. "The clear notes of," etc., *Quae . . . argutat.*   On the same
principle turn "the plaint of."
  11. Begin with *Fletne quidem an*, etc.
  12. "Anything . . . that," *quicquid*.

EXERCISE LXXXI.

TAKE, holy earth, all that my soul holds dear ;
   Take that best gift which heaven so lately gave :
To Bristol's fount I bore with trembling care
   Her faded form : she bow'd to taste the wave,

And died! Does youth, does beauty, read the line ?
  Does sympathetic fear their breasts alarm ?
Speak, dead Maria! breathe a strain divine ;
  E'en from the grave thou shalt have power to charm.
Bid them be chaste, be innocent, like thee ;
  Bid them in duty's sphere as meekly move ;
And, if so fair, from vanity as free ;
  As firm in friendship, and as fond in love.

MASON.

RETRANSLATION.

Take, Earth, what (had been) the greatest part of my
      possessions,
  Take what had been the best gift of God.
I had borne her drooping form to Bristol's fount
  In-anxiety ; she only tastes the waters with her lips,
And dies.   Does beautiful youth read this inscription ?   5
  Does prophetic fear disturb gentle hearts ?
Though-dead, Licymnia, tune a strain divine :
  In truth 'tis thine to please even from the tomb.
(Bid) that to them, as to thee, there be chaste manners
      without spot,
  Bid that they each undertake duties with as much
      docility ;   10
And (that), if there be equal beauty, there be also equal
      modesty of disposition,
  An equal loyalty in friendship and in love.

HINTS.

1, 2. The word for "what" will in each case be attracted to the
gender and number of the noun in its clause.

3. "Bristol's fount," *Bristolios fontes.* Or *Baianos* might be used.

4. "Only," *nil nisi.*

5. "And dies," *et perit.* Observe the carrying on of the sense over the end of the preceding pentameter. In this instance it makes a closer imitation of the English, but the method should be very sparingly employed.

8. "In truth," *nempe* (*nam-pe*, "why the fact is").

9. Begin with " *Ut tibi,*" and understand *ut* with *sint*, after the verb of commanding, *jube*, which ends line 10.   Comp. Ov. *Am.* i. 11. 19, "Rescribat multa jubeto."

12. "And," expressed by repeating *par* (*ā*).

EXERCISE LXXXII

LOVE is and was my Lord and King,
  And in his presence I attend
  To hear the tidings of my friend,
Which every hour his couriers bring.

Love is and was my King and Lord,
  And will be, tho' as yet I keep
  Within his court on earth, and sleep
Encompass'd by his faithful guard,

And hear at times a sentinel
  Who moves about from place to place,
  And whispers to the worlds of space
In the deep night, that all is well.

                              TENNYSON.

RETRANSLATION.

Love was my king and lord, nor has he ceased to be :
  Him I follow, to him I am-wont to be at hand (as)
    a retainer ;

And whatever is related in-his-presence about my friend,
  When a fresh messenger hurries up, is all mine.
As love was formerly lord and king over me, so both king 5
  And lord shall he be to me for all time,
Although an earthly guardianship holds me, and (my) very
  Dreams are safe with faithful attendants.
And at times I may hear as-it-were a voice,
  Where the watchman moves to and fro his silent footstep; 10
And he utters this voice through the eternal world-spaces,
  Which the void space of the world keeps revolving:
    " It is well."

HINTS.

1. "My," *mihi*.

3. "In his presence," *coram*. For the adverbial use, comp. Hor.
Sat. i. 6. 56.

5. "So," *sic*, to begin line 6.

9. "As it were," *ceu*.

10. "Silent." The word for this will end line 5.   "Moves to and
fro," *huc illuc fertque refertque*.

11. "World-spaces," *intermundia*, a term of the Epicurean philo-
sophy used by Cicero and appropriate here, though apparently not
found in verse.

12. "Keeps revolving," frequentative of *verto*.

EXERCISE LXXXIII.

TEARS, idle tears, I know not what they mean,
Tears from the depth of some divine despair
Rise in the heart and gather to the eyes,
In looking on the happy autumn-fields,
And thinking of the days that are no more.

Fresh as the first beam glittering on a sail
That brings our friends up from the underworld ;
Sad as the last which reddens over one
That sinks with all we love below the verge ;
So sad, so fresh, the days that are no more.

RETRANSLATION.

Vain indeed, nor from what fount of grief is it clear to me,
   But yet at times a tear-drop is wont to rise,
Which, drawn from the lowest recess within,
   Starts forth, and rising bedews my eyes,
When I see the plains yellow with the gift of autumn,   5
   When there return to the mind the days that have
      passed-by.
The tear-drop (is) fresh, as when in the early light a ship
   Glimmers, that is carrying (friends) returning from the
      underworld ;
(It is) sadder than the bark that now reddens in the
      western-light,
   Which the rounded billow of ocean is sinking-down.   10
So fresh are ever preserved in the remembering mind,
   So sad appear the days that have passed by.

HINTS.

1. Note that the first three lines are expanded into four in the
Latin. The odd number in each stanza of the English makes this
expedient necessary ; but which lines should be so expanded is a
matter of judgment. In the second and third stanzas the last line is
so treated, and in the fourth stanza the first line.

8. "The underworld." Comp. Virg. *Georg.* i. 240, "Mundus . . .
premitur Libyae devexus in Austros." Hence use *Devexo . . . orbe.*

10. "Is sinking-down," *deprimit.*

12. "Appear," *visi* (*sunt* being understood).

EXERCISE LXXXIV.

(*The same continued.*)

Ah, sad and strange as in dark summer dawns
The earliest pipe of half-awaken'd birds
To dying ears, when unto dying eyes
The casement slowly grows a glimmering square ;
So sad, so strange, the days that are no more.

Dear as remember'd kisses after death,
And sweet as those by hopeless fancy feign'd
On lips that are for others ; deep as love,
Deep as first love, and wild with all regret ;
O Death in Life, the days that are no more.

                                    TENNYSON.

RETRANSLATION.

As when, the darkness of summer night not yet being
        driven away,
    Birds, scarcely awakened, complain at morn,
This sounds something mournful in the ear of the dying-
        man,
    While wakeful he marks how the window grows with
        the light.
With so strange a sweetness do they touch and affect the
        feelings,   5
    So sad appear the days that have passed by.
Dear, as to a child are dear the kisses of a parent
    Whom the quiet earth holds in its cold bosom ;

Sweet, as seem those (kisses) imprinted on lips beloved
   To a despairing-one, for whom it is not granted that
      they should be his own ;   10
And impassioned as a youth who has felt first love :
   O death, not to be called life, the days that have passed
      by !

HINTS.

1. " When," *cum*, to begin line 2.

3. " Something," *nescio quid*.

5. " Touch and affect," *afficiunt captos.* See note on xxv. 8.

7. " Dear," *cara*, fem., to agree with *mors* in the last line. So with
the adjectives beginning lines 9 and 11.

10. Begin with *cui*.

12. " Not to be called," *parum.*

EXERCISE LXXXV.

CALM is the morn without a sound,
    Calm as to suit a calmer grief,
    And only thro' the faded leaf
The chestnut pattering to the ground :

Calm and deep peace on this high wold,
    And on these dews that drench the furze,
    And all the silvery gossamers
That twinkle into green and gold :

Calm and still light on yon great plain
    That sweeps with all its autumn bowers,
    And crowded farms and lessening towers,
To mingle with the bounding main :

Calm and deep peace in this wide air,
These leaves that redden to the fall;
And in my heart, if calm at all,
If any calm, a calm despair.

TENNYSON.

RETRANSLATION.

In the morning the breezes are still; no sound breaks the
repose,
Such (repose) as settled grief might have.
All-things-alike are still, save-that through the dry leaves
with frequent fall
The chestnuts are hastening to come-to-the ground.
Deep repose holds these elevated spaces of the high
plain,   5
(And) these dews, with which the bushes besprent are
wet;
These webs that the spider lightly stretches on the
shrubs,
Which twinkle now with green, now with golden
light.
Behold the plains smiling in the still light
Behold (the tracts) hidden from the light by foliage
sere;   10
See the gables of farm-houses and the distant towers,
Where the sea bounds the far-stretching lands.
Deep peace tranquillizes these regions of the wide air;
The forest is still, soon to be widowed of its yellow
leaves.
And if aught of calm is in my breast, if any peace   15
Holds (it), shattered hope has given me peace.

HINTS.

2. "Might," *possit*; the subjunctive expressing the generalizing force of "such as to suit." See note on lxxiv. 2.

4. "To come to the ground," *praecipitare*. For the intransitive usage comp. Virg. *Aen.* ix. 670.

6. "Are wet," *maduere*.

7. "Lightly," adj. See note on xxix. 1.

8. Use *qui* in both clauses, but *modo* only in the second.

10. "Tracts," inserted only to indicate the neuter plural of the adjective.

12. "Far-stretching," *procul extentos*.

15. "Calm," adj.   "Any," to begin line 16.

EXERCISE LXXXVI.

THERE rolls the deep where grew the tree.
> O earth, what changes hast thou seen !
> There, where the long street roars, hath been
The stillness of the central sea.

The hills are shadows, and they flow
> From form to form, and nothing stands ;
> They melt like mist, the solid lands,
Like clouds they shape themselves and go.

But in my spirit will I dwell,
> And dream my dream, and hold it true ;
> For though my lips may breathe adieu,
I cannot think the thing farewell.

TENNYSON.

RETRANSLATION.

Here rolls the deep sea, where the tree had grown :
> What changes it has been given thee, Earth, to undergo !

M

Where the long street hums with the people, aforetime
   There has been here deep stillness in the midst of the
      waves.
Like a shadow, the mountains change and assume forms   5
   Ever new : nothing in the world stands fixed.
Though stable, the earth melts like a mist,
   Or passes-away made-like to watery clouds.
But be it allowed me to wrap myself always in my own mind,
   And to imagine in dreams things that I may think true
      for me.   10
For though I be able to utter this word with unwilling lips,
   I apprehend not what that *thing*, Farewell ! doth mean.

HINTS.

   1. " Rolls," *fluctuat.*
   3. " Hums," *circumstrepit.*
   6. " Stands," *constat.*
   8 " Made like," *assimulata*
   9 " To wrap." Comp. Hor *Carm.* iii. 29. 54, " Virtute me in-
volvo."
   10. " Things that," *quae.*
   11. " Though," *ut.*

EXERCISE LXXXVII.

St. Agnes' Eve.

   Deep on the convent-roof the snows
      Are sparkling to the moon :
   My breath to heaven like vapour goes :
      May my soul follow soon !
   The shadows of the convent-towers
      Slant down the snowy sward,

Still creeping with the creeping hours
    That lead me to my Lord.
Make Thou my spirit pure and clear
    As are the frosty skies,
Or this first snowdrop of the year
    That in my bosom lies.

RETRANSLATION.

Deep on the roof of the sacred temple lies the snow,
    And sparkles undefiled in the rays of the moon ;
Like a vapour, the breath vanishes into the thin air :
    O would that I might myself soon quickly follow !
And now the shadow falls slanting from the lofty towers, 5
    Where the ground lies hidden, white with the snow
        spread-over-it,
And creeps-on along with the hours creeping-on,
    By which I am being drawn towards my Lord, to-be
        his bride.
May God make me devoid of fault, and free from stain,
    And like the expanse of the cold sky ;   10
White as is the floweret of the opening year,
    That lies drooping in the midst of my bosom.

HINTS.

1. "On," *super*, "lies," *incubat.*
3. "Vanishes," *rarescit.*
4. "Soon," *posita . . . mora.*
9. "Make," to come in line 10. For each "and" in this sentence
use *me* in the Latin, the pronoun being repeated.
10. "Expanse," *templa.* Compare the "caeli caerula templa " of
Ennius. The word properly means a portion cut off, hence a space.
12. "Drooping," *pensilis.*

EXERCISE LXXXVIII.

(The same continued.)

As these white robes are soil'd and dark
  To yonder shining ground ;
As this pale taper's earthly spark,
  To yonder argent round ;
So shows my soul before the Lamb,
  My spirit before Thee ;
So in mine earthly house I am,
  To that I hope to be.
Break up the heavens, O Lord ! and far,
  Through all yon starlight keen,
Draw me, thy bride, a glittering star,
  In raiment white and clean.

RETRANSLATION.

As this robe, though it has been most bright, is dull,
  And seems black by-the-side-of the snowy ground ;
As this lamp burns pale with earthly flame,
  And darts its rays more feebly than the orb of the
    moon ;
So my spirit, when it is laid bare before the eternal Lamb, 5
  Is offered not without spot to thee :
So to me, since I am enclosed in a bodily form,
  The power is not yet given of living in such guise as
    I shall be.

Burst open, O God, the marvellous palaces of the spacious
      heaven,
  And bear me through the lights of the starry sky !   10
A glittering star may I, thy bride, be borne aloft on high,
  And be attired in a covering of snow-white robes.

HINTS.

1. "Is dull," *sordet.*

4. "More feebly," *segnius.*

5. "Spirit," to come in line 6.

7. "Enclosed," *circumdata.*

8. "The power is not yet given," *nondum . . . posse datur,* with
an infinitive. "In such guise as," *qualis.*

12. End with *corpus amicta tegar,* which cannot well be literally
translated. The word for "robes" will be in the ablative

EXERCISE LXXXIX.

(The same continued.)

HE lifts me to the golden doors ;
  The flashes come and go ;
All heaven bursts her starry floors,
  And strows her lights below,
And deepens on and up ! the gates
  Roll back, and far within
For me the Heavenly Bridegroom waits,
  To make me pure of sin.
The Sabbaths of Eternity,
  One Sabbath deep and wide—
A light upon the shining sea—
  The Bridegroom with his bride !
TENNYSON.

RETRANSLATION.

Oh! I am in ecstasy : now (I see) heaven open its golden
    gates,
  Now I see the ruddy torch-lights come and go :
Lo ! the floor of heaven lies open, its pavements burst,
  And a thousand stars glitter, strewn beneath my feet.
Clearer and higher still the light goes rushing on; the very 5
  Gates are unbarred, God himself is seen.
He, awaiting his Bride, is sitting within the court above,
  To wash-away all guilt from my soul.
Now (there is) eternal rest, now the leisure of deep peace,
  A leisure, that no length of time can break ;   10
(There is) light shed-abroad over the calm face of ocean,
  (And) a spouse evermore the consolation of his spouse.

HINTS.

1. Begin with "Labor, io !" (comp. Tibull. ii. 4. 6), to soften the
abruptness of transition in language of excitement.

2. "Come and go," *ire redire.*

5. "Goes rushing on," *ingruit.*

7. "Within the court," lit. "innermost in the court." So *medius*
is often used. "Above" will be expressed by an adjective in agreement with *aula.*

9. "Leisure," *otia* (pl.) "That no length of time can break,"
quae nequeat, etc., longa dies. For the subjunctive see note on lxxiv. 2.
When is *dies* feminine ?

EXERCISE XC.

THE REAPER AND THE FLOWERS.

THERE is a Reaper, whose name is Death ;
　　And with his sickle keen
He reaps the bearded grain at a breath,
　　And the flowers that grow between.

"Shall I have nought that is fair ?" saith he ;
　　"Have nought but the bearded grain ?
Though the breath of these flowers is sweet to me,
　　I will give them all back again."

He gazed at the flowers with tearful eyes,
　　He kissed their drooping leaves ;
It was for the Lord of Paradise
　　He bound them in his sheaves.

RETRANSLATION.

There is one of the reapers whom they call Death,
　　Applying his sickle-bearing hands to the joyous standing-
　　　　corn ;
Untiringly cuts he down the bristling ears with his steel,
　　And gathers the corn, not without flowers intermingled.
"Am I to reap nothing of a fairer kind ?" saith he,　　5
　　"To fill my bosom with a harvest of grain alone ?
All the flowers that I give back smell sweetly,
　　Yet I would fain restore these when cut."
And so he gazed-at the flowers with starting tears,
　　And gave many a kiss to their drooping leaves :　　10

He is preparing garlands, binding (them) in the sheaf of
   corn,
   To-be an acceptable gift for God that-dwelleth-in-
      heaven.

HINTS.

1. Begin with the relative. " One of," *unus*, following *de* with
ablative.

3. "Steel," lit. "edge," *acies*.

4. "Flowers ;" use the singular.

5. "Am I," etc. This form of indignant question, or exclamation,
is expressed by the accusative of the pronoun and the infinitive, or by
the nominative of the pronoun and *ut* with the subjunctive. Comp.
Virg. *Aen.* i. 37. "Of a fairer kind," *quod sit speciosius.* For the
subjunctive, see note on lxxvii. 9.

6. "Of grain " (lit. "wheat "), *triticeus*, adj.

7. "All . . . that," *quodcumque*, with genitive.

8. "Would fain," *velim*, with perf. inf. " When cut," *accisos*,
lit. "cut at," "half cut through."

10. "Many a," *multa* (pl.) The *que* in this clause will come
later than second word.

11. "Sheaf of corn." Comp. Virg. *Georg.* ii. 516, " cerealis mergite
culmi."

12. "To be," fut. partic. " That dwelleth in heaven," *caelicolae*.

EXERCISE XCI.

(*The same continued.*)

" MY Lord has need of these flowerets gay,"
   The Reaper said, and smiled :
" Dear tokens of the earth are they,
   Where he was once a child.

"They shall all bloom in fields of light,
　　Transplanted by my care,
And saints upon their garments white
　　These sacred blossoms wear."

LONGFELLOW.

RETRANSLATION.

"There is need of that flower," smiling gently he says ;
　"God requires those garlands to be delivered to himself :
They are to him sweet memorials of the former life,
　In which he grew among children, himself too a child.
Where the Lord sows his fields, with suns ever-shining, 5
　My care will sprinkle these with celestial water :
They who have made their garments white by the death
　　of Christ
Will bear (them) whitening on a still-whiter bosom."

HINTS.

4. "Child," *puer.*
5. "Ever-shining," *assiduus.*   Comp. Lucr. v. 253.
6. "Sprinkle," *rigo.*
7. "By the death of Christ," *Christo . . . caeso.*
8. "Whitening," *candentes.*

EXERCISE XCII.

RETIREMENT.

FAR from the world, O Lord, I flee,
　　From strife and tumult far,
From scenes where Satan wages still
　　His most successful war.

The calm retreat, the silent shade
　With prayer and praise agree;
And seem by thy sweet bounty made
　For those who follow thee.

There, if thy Spirit teach the soul,
　And grace her mean abode,
Oh! with what peace, and joy, and love
　She communes with her God!

RETRANSLATION.

Far from the din of the crowd, O merciful Father,
　Where strifes and many a brawl harass the mind, I am
　　borne;
And I shun the streets, where Satan prompts crimes,
　And displays his arms victorious in his own camp.
Shady vales and tranquil country-places　　　　　　　5
　Afford a spot ever prepared for thy praise and for
　　prayers;
And all things own thee (as) their author, in order that
　　for those
　Who keep thy laws, rest may there be present.
Oh! if thy Spirit here breathes at times upon my soul,
　And deigns to ennoble her humble dwelling,　　　10
How great love, how great peace and joys refresh the mind,
　When it feels that here it has God (for) its companion.

HINTS.

1. "Merciful Father," *Pater Optime*.
2. "The mind," at end of line 1.
3. "Satan," *Sătănăs*.
6. "Prepared," at end of line 5.

EXERCISE XCIII.

(*The same continued.*)

THERE, like the nightingale she pours
    Her solitary lays ;
Nor asks a witness of her song,
    Nor thirsts for human praise.

Author and guardian of my life,
    Sweet source of light divine,
And—all harmonious names in one—
    My Saviour ! thou art mine.

What thanks I owe thee, and what love,
    A boundless, endless store,
Shall echo through the realms above,
    When time shall be no more.

COWPER.

RETRANSLATION.

Here, like the nightingale under the deep shade of the
        groves,
    She delights to pour in solitude her sweet strains ;
Nor asks that any one should be near her (as) a witness
        of the song,
    Nor thirsts here for the honour that popular applause
        brings.
O benign guardian and author of my life, and also   5
    The source whence divine light comes to my soul,

And (that my strain may join whatever is lovable in one
  Name), Saviour! it is granted that thou shouldst be
  mine.
What praises my grateful soul would fain pour forth to
  thee,
  How boundless is the love which it owes thee,   10
My voice shall sing resounding through the realms of
  heaven, when
  The fleeting shadow shall no longer divide the day.

HINTS.

2. " In solitude," *sola.*

4. " Popular applause," *populi* . . . *aura.* Comp. Hor. *Carm.* iii.
2. 20, " arbitrio popularis aurae." The verb will be in the subj., for
the same reason as in lxxiv. 2.

5. " And also," *et idem.* This use of *idem* (lit. " the same ")
should be noticed. Comp. Virg. *Aen.* viii. 290, ix. 327.

9. " Would fain," *vellet.*

EXERCISE XCIV.

GRACE AND PROVIDENCE.

ALMIGHTY God, whose wondrous hand
Supports the weight of sea and land ;
Whose grace is such a boundless store,
No heart shall break that sighs for more ;

Thy providence supplies my food,
And 'tis thy blessing makes it good ;
My soul is nourish'd by thy word :
Let soul and body praise the Lord !

My streams of outward comfort came
From him who built this earthly frame ;
Whate'er I want his bounty gives,
By whom my soul for ever lives.

RETRANSLATION.

Almighty Lord of the universe, who the weight (*acc.*) of earth
And the vast waters dost hold with marvellous hand,
And, if a suppliant breast sends to thee its sighs,
   Whose grace pours-forth unexhausted riches ;
Thou dost providently fill my table with bread and viands ;   5
And 'tis of-thee that food renews my limbs with strength.
Nourishment (*pl.*) to the soul (thy) heavenly word supplies;
   Let body and soul themselves pay thanks to God.
He who gave these earthly members, delights to add
   The blessings which, like an ever-flowing stream, sustain me.   10
He with bountiful hand bestows all things that are wanting,
   And gives to my soul happy days without death.

HINTS.

1. "Universe," *res* (pl.)
5. "Providently ;" see note on xxix. 1.   "My," *mihi.*
6. "'Tis of thee," *tuum est,* which may end the line.
8. "Body," *membra.*
10. "Like," *more,* with genitive.   Note the transposition of lines 9 and 10 in the original.
11. "He," *ille,* being emphatic.

EXERCISE XCV.

(The same continued.)

EITHER his hand preserves from pain,
Or, if I feel it, heals again;
From Satan's malice shields my breast,
Or overrules it for the best.

Forgive the song that falls so low
Beneath the gratitude I owe!
It means the praise, however poor:—
An angel's song can do no more.

COWPER.

RETRANSLATION.

His right-hand either keeps far-off every pain,
    Or else, if I am at all in pain, a source of safety is-at-
        hand.
He wards-off from me the malicious darts of Satan, and
        to good (things)
    Loves to turn all the evils that are likely-to-harm.
Grant pardon to a muse which, when a grateful soul   5
    Wishes to utter sublime strains, creeps on-the-ground.
Great Father, it seeks to extol thy praises:
    A heavenly voice is-unable to speak better-things.

HINTS.

1. "Keeps far off," *procul arcet.*
2. "If . . . at all," *si quid.*

3. "Satan," *Sătănas*, genitive *-ae.* " To good things," *bonis-que.* The use of the dative may perhaps be justified by Virgil's *ut clamor caelo.* Otherwise, the usual construction of *vertere* is *in* (more rarely *ad*) with the accusative

4. " All . . . that," *quotquot.*

5, 6. The word for " soul " comes in line 6, and for " sublime " in line 5.

7. " It " (*i e* the Muse) *illa.*

EXERCISE XCVI.

EPITAPH, 1666.

SHE on this clayen pillow layed her head,
. As brides do use the first to go to bed.
He missed her soone, and yet ten months he trys
To live apart, and likes it not, and dyes.

RETRANSLATION.

With neck supported on a clayey pillow she reclines,
As when a new bride goes to her first couch (*pl.*).
He felt that his (loved one) was gone ; but in the tenth month, forlorn
When he would not live, he preferred himself to die.

HINTS.

1. " With neck," etc., lit. "supported as to neck." In what case does the Latin express this "nearer definition," or "part affected"?

3. " Was gone," *abesse.*

4. " Would not." Is " would " here a mere auxiliary, or does it imply *will ?*

EXERCISE XCVII.

"ABIDE WITH US."

WHEN the soft dews of kindly sleep
My wearied eyelids gently steep,
Be my last thought, how sweet to rest
For ever on my Saviour's breast.

Abide with me from morn till eve,
For without thee I cannot live ;
Abide with me when night is nigh,
For without thee I dare not die.

Thou Framer of the light and dark,
Steer through the tempest thine own ark :
Amid the howling wintry sea
We are in port, if we have thee.

RETRANSLATION.

As often as, like dew most welcome to the weary grass,
    Kindly repose steeps my drooping eyes,
Be that the latest care of my mind, how much
    Sweeter (it is) to be ever in the bosom of the Lord.
From the rising of the suns to the hours of evening do
        thou with me
    Ever be present, for without thee I cannot live.
Do thou (be present) with me, when at length night has
        brought-on the late shadows,
    For without thee, my only hope, I fear to die.

Do thou, who madest both the darkness and the confines
   of light,
  Thyself guard thy bark amid the stormy waters: 10
Both amid the wintry waves and the perils of the sea
   A haven is-at-hand (for him) to whom God will be pro-
   pitious.

HINTS.

1. Begin with *Me quotiens;* the accusative *oculos* in the next line being one of nearer definition.

3. "That," *illa,* in agreement with *cura.*

4. "To be in," *inesse.*

5. Begin with *Tu mihi.* "From the rising of," *post ortos.*

6. "Be present,"—at the end of the line.   What forms has the pres. imper. of *adsum?*

7. "Has brought-on," fut. perf.

12. "Will be," *velit esse.*   Comp. xcvi. 4.

EXERCISE XCVIII.

(The same continued.)

WATCH by the sick ; enrich the poor
With blessings from thy boundless store :
Be every mourner's sleep to night
Like infant's slumbers, pure and light.

Come near and bless us when we wake,
Ere through the world our course we take ;
Till in the ocean of thy love
We lose ourselves in heaven above.

KEBLE.

N

RETRANSLATION.

Sit-by the sick-man's bed : let the poor-man thy gifts
    Receive,—gifts sent with a liberal hand.
Let gentle slumbers this night welcome the mourner,
    Such as (is) the soft and deep repose in an infant.
In the morning be present, and bless (us) rising with peace-
        ful countenance,   5
    That the day newly-begun may go forth with favourable
        omens ;
Until, sunk in full tide of bliss as in an ocean,
    That love of-thine upbear us to the choirs above.

HINTS.

1. "Sit-by," pres. subj.

5. "Bless :" comp. Virg *Georg.* i. 40, "audacibus annue coeptis."

6. "Day newly-begun," *nova lux.* This line ends with a quadri-syllable.

7. "Sunk," acc. plu., agreeing with *nos* in the next line. "In full tide of bliss," *multa dulcedine.*

EXERCISE XCIX.

ABIDE with me ; fast falls the eventide ;
The darkness deepens ; Lord, with me abide.
When other helpers fail, and comforts flee,
Help of the helpless, O abide with me.

Swift to its close ebbs out life's little day ;
Earth's joys grow dim, its glories pass away ;
Change and decay in all around I see :
O thou who changest not, abide with me.

I need thy presence every passing hour ;
What but thyself can foil the tempter's power ?

Who like thyself my guide and stay can be?
Through cloud and sunshine, Lord, abide with me.

RETRANSLATION.

Christ, abide with me ! now does evening overshadow the
  earth ;
 The shades thicken ; do thou, O God, ever remain.
Companions will fail, the comforts of life will flee :—
 O helper of the helpless, be thou always near me.
As an ebbing wave, the life of men swiftly glides ;   5
 Joys vanish, every honour falls ;
Whatever I behold, shifts and changes hourly :
 With me, O unconscious of change, do thou ever remain.
I need thee (as) a guide, present through all hours :
 Who, save thee, could restrain the violence of Satan ? 10
Who will be a defence and protection to us, like thee ?
 Whether the sky is favourable, or a storm rages, be present.

HINTS.

  1. "Overshadow," *inumbro*.
  7. "Shifts," *fluit*.
  10. "Could," *queat* or *valet*.
  11. Begin with *par tibi*.

EXERCISE C.

(*The same continued.*)

I FEAR no foe, with thee at hand to bless ;
Ills have no weight, and tears no bitterness ;
Where is Death's sting ? where, Grave, thy victory ?
I triumph still, if thou abide with me.

Hold thou thy cross before my closing eyes ;
Shine through the gloom, and point me to the skies ;
Heaven's morning breaks, and earth's vain shadows flee :
In life, in death, O Lord, abide with me.

LYTE.

RETRANSLATION.

Secure in such protection neither could foe affright,
    Nor tears pain, nor hard lot oppress :
It is not bitter to die ; no longer will Orcus bear sway ;
    Death being triumphed-over, under thy guidance, I
        shall be victorious.
Do thou uplift thy standard before the eyes of (me)
        dying, to the stars   5
That I may soar on shining path, thou going before :
When divine light shall have scattered the shades of earth,
    Through life and death do thou, O God, ever remain.

HINTS.

1. "Protection," *auspicium.* "Could affright," pres. subj. The subjunctive, as thus used, *in apodosi,* when the conditional clause is not expressed, but implied, is sometimes called the conjunctive mood.

2. "Hard," *iniqua.*

3. " Bitter," *crudele.*

4. " Being triumphed over," *triumphata.*

7. " Of earth," *terrenas.*

VOCABULARY.

. *This Vocabulary is not meant to supersede the use of a Dictionary, but only to be a guide for the words to be used, which should then be looked out, where necessary, in a Latin-English Dictionary.*

Abandon, dēstǐtuo, -ere.
Able, to be, possum, pŏtui.
Above, sŭpra ; from above, dē-sŭper.
Absent, to be, absum, ǎbesse.
Accord, of its own, spontĕ ; ultrŏ (the latter implying "being the first to," "going the length of").
Accustomed, to be, sŏleo, -ere, sŏlǐtus sum.
Add, to, addo, -ĕre.
Admire, to, miror, -ari ; admǐror, -arı.
Admit of, to, = suffer, pătior, pătı.
Adorn, to, dĕcŏro, -are ; orno, -are.
Advance, to, prŏcēdo, -ere.
Affair, an, rēs, rĕi.
Affection, amor, -ōrıs.
Again (of repetition), ǐtĕrum ; = back again, rursus.
Age = time of life, aetas, -ātis ; = generation, saecŭlum.
Aged woman, ǎnus.

Ah ! *a*, sometimes *at*.
Air (lower) āēr, -ĕris ; (upper) aethĕr, -ĕris.
Alas ! heu, ĕheu. (As in Plautus and Terence, ĕheu is found, some editors prefer heu, heu when a spondee is required. But see Orelli's note on Hor. *Sat.* 1. 3 66.)
All, omnis (pl.) ; cunctus (pl.) ; all the = the whole, totus.
Alone, sōlus.
Already, jam.
Also, ĕtiam, quŏque.
Amid, inter (with *acc.*)
Among, sometimes *in* with *abl.* See amid.
Anchor, ancŏra.
Ancient, antīquus.
And, ĕt, āc, ātque, -quĕ.
Anger, ira.
Annals, fasti, -ōrum.
Anon, mŏdŏ.
Another, ǎlius (*gen.* ǎlīus).
Another (of two) alter.
Anticipate, to, praecǐpio, -ĕre.

Anxious, sollĭcĭtus, anxius;
anxiety, maestĭtĭa.
Any, ullus; with ne, si, etc.,
quis, *fem.* quă.
Applause, plausus.
Apple, pōmum, mālum (both
general terms; the former in-
cluding stone fruit, the latter
not).
Approach, to, accēdo, -ere; ădeo,
-ire, prŏpius ire.
Arise, to, ŏrior, ŏrīri, ortus;
surgo, -ere.
Arm (of the body) brāchium,
lăcertus.
Arms = armour, arma, -orum (*n.
pl.*)
Art, ars, artis.
As, nt; ceu; vĕlut; velŭti; tam-
quam; non sĕcus ac; as if, quăsĭ.
As often as, quŏtiens.
Associate, to, sŏcĭo, -are; con-
socio, -are.
At once, ilĭcet.
Attachment, fĭdes.
Autumn, autumnus; autumnal,
autumnālis.
Avail, to, văleo, -ere.
Azure, caerŭlus, caerŭleus.

Backwards, rĕtro.
Bad, mălus.
Band, chŏrus.
Bank (of a river), rĭpa.
Bark (of a tree), cortex, -ĭcis; =
ship, rătis.
Bay (tree) laurus; of bay, laureus.
Bear, to, fĕro, ferre, tŭli, lātum.
Bear to, affĕro; borne to, allā-
tus; upbear, sustĭneo, -ere.

Beautiful, formōsus, pulcer.
Become, to, dēceo, -ere; becom-
ing, dĕcens; = to grow, fio,
fĭĕri.
Bed, cŭbile, -is; tŏrus.
Before, ante (with *acc.*); = ere,
antĕquam; priusquam.
Beguile, dēcĭpio, -ere, fallo, -ere.
Behold, to, adspĭcio, -ĕre.
Believe, crēdo, -ere.
Beloved, ămātus, cārus.
Below, infra; from below, sur-
sum.
Bend, to, inclīno, -are; flecto,
-ere; bend over, incŭbo, -are
(*dat.*)
Beneath, sŭb (*abl.* of position;
acc. of motion).
Bereave, to, orbo, -are.
Beside, praeter; juxtā.
Besides, praetĕrĕā.
Bewail, to, plōro, -are; lūgeo,
-ere.
Bind, to, implĭco, -are, -ui; necto,
-ere; vincio, -ire.
Bird, ăvis; ālĕs, -ĭtis; volŭcris.
Black, āter; nĭger (glossy black).
Blade, ensis.
Blast, flāmen, -ĭnis.
Blended, mistus.
Blood, sanguis, -ĭnis; (when shed)
cruor, -ōris.
Blood-stained, crŭentus.
Blush, to, rŭbesco.
Boar, wild-boar, ăper, -pri.
Body, corpus, -ŏris.
Bond, vincŭlum, vinclum.
Bone, ŏs, ossis.
Born, nātus.
Bosom, grĕmium; = lap, sĭnus.

Both (together), ambo; (separately) ûtrique.

Bough, rāmus; brācchium.

Boundless, immensus.

Bow, arcus.

Boy, puer; **boyish**, puĕrĭlis.

Branch, rāmus.

Break, rumpo, -ere; = **snap**, frango, -ere; (*intr.* = to be broken), rumpi.

Breast, pectus, -ōris.

Breath, spīrĭtus.

Breathe, to, spīro, -are; **breathe out**, exhālo, -are; efflo, -are.

Breeze, aura.

Bright, clārus; praeclarus; sometimes purpŭreus, candĭdus.

Bring, to, fĕro; affĕro, -erre, **bring back**, rĕfĕro.

Brother, frāter, -tris.

Brow = forehead, frons, frontis; tempŏra (*pl.*); = **eyebrow**, sŭpercĭlium.

Bubble, bulla.

Burden, ŏnus, -ĕris.

Burn, to, ardeo, -ere.

Burst, to, rumpo, -ere; **burst forth** (*intr.*), ērumpo

But, sed; at; ast (before vowel, if wanted long).

Cable, vincŭlum, vinclum.

Call, vŏco, -are; **call back**, rĕvoco.

Can (see **able, to be**); cannot, nĕqueo, -ire; nescio, -ire.

Care, cūra; **careful**, sēdŭlus.

Career, cursus.

Carry, porto, -are; **carry off**, tollo, sustŭli; aufĕro, abstŭli.

Catch, căpio, -ĕre; = **intercept**, excĭpio, -ĕre.

Cedar, cĕdrus.

Chance, cāsus; sors, sortis.

Chaplet, cŏrōna, cŏrolla.

Chase, to, exăgĭto, -are.

Cheek, gĕna.

Child, infans.

City, urbs, urbis.

Cleave, sĕco, -are; scindo, -ere.

Climb, to, scando, -ere; ascendo.

Close, to, claudo, -ere; occlūdo (=shut in face of).

Close by, prŏpĕ; juxta.

Cold (*s.*), frĭgus, -ŏris.

Cold (*adj.*), frĭgĭdus.

Come, to, vĕnio, -ire; **come forth**, exeo; prodeo, -ire; **come over**, subeo, -ire.

Commerce, mercātūra.

Companion, cŏmes, -ĭtis; sŏcius.

Complaint, quĕrēla; questus.

Comrade, cŏmes, -ĭtis.

Contest, certāmen, -ĭnis.

Convey together, convĕho, -ere.

Cornfield (*lit.* crop), sĕgĕs, -ĕtis.

Corpse, corpus; cădāver; fūnus.

Could. See **able, to be**.

Council, concĭlium; **counsel**, consĭlium.

Countenance, ōs, ōris, *pl.* ōra; vultus.

Countless, innŭmĕrus.

Country (fatherland), pătria.

Country (opposed to town), rūs, rūris.

Course, cursus.

Cover, to, tĕgo, -ere; condo, -ere.

Covering, tegmen, -ĭnis.

Crack, to, frango, -ere.

Creak, to, strīdeo, -ere.

Crown, cŏrōna ; cŏrolla ; king's crown, diădēma.

Cruel, crūdēlis.

Cry, clāmo, -are ; conclamo ; exclamo.

Cut, to, sĕco, -are ; cut down, dēcīdo, -ere.

Dance, to, mŏveor, -eri ; salto, -are.

Dare, to, audeo, -ere, ausus sum.

Day, dīes ; always m. in pl. ; fem. in sing. when it = time, or when it means an appointed day ; to-day, hŏdiē.

Deadly, lētĭfer.

Dear, cārus, ămātus.

Death, mors, mortis ; lētum ; fūnus, -ĕris.

Deed, factum ; fácĭnus, -ŏris.

Deep, altus, prŏfundus ; of sounds, grăvis.

Deity, nūmen, -ĭnis.

Depart, to, discēdo, -ere ; ăbeo, -ire.

Depend, hang from, dēpendeo, -ere.

Depth (of the sea), gurgĕs, -ĭtis ; altum ; prŏfundum.

Desert = deserving, mĕrĭtum.

Deserted, dēsertus, rĕlĭctus.

Deserve, to, mĕreor, -ēri ; deserving, merĭtus ; not deserving, immĕrĭtus.

Despair, to, despēro, -are ; in despair, desperans.

Destined to, often a sign of the fut. partic.

Destruction, exĭtium.

Dew, rōs, rōris.

Die, to, mŏrior, mŏri, mortuus.

Die away, to, dēpĕreo, -ire.

Different, dīversus ; ălius.

Disdain, to, dēdĭgnor, -ari.

Dismiss, to, dīmitto, -ere.

Dissension, sĭmultas, -ātis ; dissĭdium ; discordia.

Distant, longinquus ; rĕmōtus.

Distinction, hŏnor, -ōris.

Distracted, āmens.

Do, to, ăgo, -ere ; făcĭo, -ere ; 'tis done! actum est.

Door, jānua ; doors, fŏres.

Dove, cŏlumba.

Downfall, ruīna.

Draw, to, trăho, -ere ; draw off, or away, dētraho.

Droop, to, langueo, -ere ; drooping, languĭdus.

Drop, gutta.

Dry, siccus, ārĭdus ; dry ground, siccum.

Dutiful, pius.

Dwelling, tectum, lăres (pl.)

Each (of two), ŭterque ; each one, quisque.

Early, priscus ; prīmaevus.

Edge, ăcies, -ēi.

Efface, to, dēleo, -ere.

Embrace (s.), amplexus, complexus.

Embrace, to, amplector, -ti.

Emotion, mōtus (lit. movement) ; animi (pl.)

Encircle, to, cingo, -ere.

Endure, dūro, -are

England, Anglia.

Engrave, insculpo, -ere.

Enjoy, to, fruor, frui (with *abl.*); carpo, -ere (*acc.*)

Ennoble, to, nōbĭlĭto, -are.

Enrich, to, dīto, -are; enriched (of land), pinguis.

Ensue, to, fīo, fĭĕri ; sĕquor, -quī.

Equal, pār, pāris.

Ere, antĕquam; prĭusquam : the two parts of each word may be separated.

Escape, to, fŭgio, -ĕre, fŭgi (*pf.*); effŭgio

Even (*adv.*), vel, et, etiam; even so, haud alĭter, etc. See So.

Evening, vesper, -ĕris; at evening, vespertinus (*adj.*)

Ever = always, semper; = at any time, unquam; evermore, usque.

Every, omnis (*sing.*); every one, quisque, generally with personal or possessive pronoun, as quisque sĭbi, and verb in plural.

Expressiveness, fācundia.

Exult, to, exsulto, -are.

Eye, ŏcŭlus; ŏcellus; lūmen, -ĭnis.

Face, ōs, ōris, ōra (*pl.*); fācĭes; vultus.

Fade, to, marceo, -ere.

Faint (of sound), tĕnuis; = drooping, languĭdus.

Fair, candĭdus; dĕcōrus. See beautiful.

Faithful, fīdus, fīdēlis.

Faithless, infīdus.

Fall, to, cădo, -ere; occĭdo, -ere; ready to fall, cădūcus.

Fame, fāma.

Familiar, nōtus.

Far, prŏcul, longē.

Farewell, vălē (*sing.*), vălētĕ (*pl.*)

Favourable, sĕcundus; faustus.

Father, păter, pătris; gĕnĭtor, -ōris.

Feel, to, sentio, -ire; feeling, conscius.

Field, ăger, ăgri; arvum; culta (*pl.*)

Fill, to, impleo; compleo, -ēre.

First, primus.

Fix, to, constĭtuo, -ĕre.

Flag, vexillum.

Flattery, blandītia, usually in *pl.*

Flee, or fly, to, fŭgio, -ĕre.

Fleet, classis.

Flickering, trĕmŭlus.

Fling, on or about, to, injĭcio, -ĕre, with *dat.*

Flow, to, fluo, -ere; flow past, praefluo.

Flower, flōs, flōris; flowery, flōrens; flōrĭdus.

Flushed, flăgrans, -ntis.

Fly (as a bird), to, vŏlo, -are.

Foam, spūma; foamy, spūmeus.

Foliage, cŏmae (*pl.*)

Follow, to, sĕquor, sĕqui, sĕcūtus.

Foot, pēs, pĕdis; footstep, pēs; passus; vestĭgium; planta.

For (*conj.*) nam; ĕnim.

For = in return for, pro.

Force, vis (no *gen.* or *dat.*); in *pl.* = strength.

Forehead, frons, frontis.

Foreign, externus, ălĭēnus.

Forgetful, immĕmor, oblītus, both with *gen.*

Forsake, dēsĕro, -ere; destĭtuo, -ere.

Forsworn, perjūrus.

Fortune, fortūna.

Fostering, altrix, -icis (*fem. adj.*)

Fountain, fons, fontis.

Fragrant, ŏdōrus ; ŏdōrātus ; frăgrans.

Frail, frăgĭlĭs.

Frame (*lit.* bones), ossa (*n. pl.*)

Frame, to, fingo, -ere

Fraternity, sŏdălĭtium.

Fresh, rĕcens, also used adverbially.

Friend, ămīcus ; friendly, ămīcus.

Friendship, ămīcĭtĭa.

From, ă, ăb ; = out of, ē, ex.

Full, plēnus.

Funeral, fūnus, -ĕris.

Gale, flābrum ; flāmen, -ĭnĭs.

Garden, hortus.

Garland, sertum ; cŏrōna ; cŏrolla.

Gaul, Gallĭa.

Gem, gemma.

Gentle, mollis, lēnis.

Give, to, do, dăre, dĕdi, dătum.

Glassy, vĭtreus.

Glide, to, lābor, -i, lapsus.

Gloomy, āter (*lit.* black) ; tristis.

Glory, glōria ; dĕcus, -ŏris.

Glow, to, ardeo.

Go, eo, ire , go away, ăbeo, -īre ; go by, praetĕreo ; go to, accēdo.

God, deus, *voc.* deus, *nom. pl.* di.

Godlike, dīvīnus.

Gold, aurum ; golden, aureus.

Good, bŏnus ; bŏnum (*subst.*)

Grace, gracefulness, grātia.

Grant, to, do, dăre ; praebeo, -ere.

Grave, sĕpulcrum.

Great, magnus ; grandis ; how great, what great, quantus ; quam magnus.

Grief = smart, dŏlor ; = mourning, luctus.

Grieve for, to, dŏleo, -ere (*acc.*)

Ground, sŏlum, hŭmus ; on the ground, hŭmi.

Grow, to, cresco, -ĕre ; = to become, fio, fĭĕri.

Guilty, scĕlĕrātus.

Hand, mănus ; dextera, dextra (*lit.* right hand) ; at hand, to be, adsum, ădesse.

Handmaid, serva ; ancilla ; mĭnistra.

Hang, to, pendeo, -ēre (*intr.*) ; pendo, -ĕre (*trans.*) Both make perfect pĕpendi.

Harass, to, prĕmo, -ere ; vexo, -are ; exerceo, -ere.

Harbinger, nuntius, nuntia.

Hard, dūrus ; hard by, ad ; juxtā.

Harm, damnum ; fraus.

Haste, to, propero, -are.

Have, to, hăbeo, -ere.

Haven, portus.

Head, căput, -ĭtis.

Heal, to, sāno, -are.

Hear, to, audio, -ire.

Heart, cŏr, cordĭs ; pectus, -ŏris, pectora (*pl.*)

Hearth, fŏcus.

Heat, ardor, -ōris ; văpor, -ōris.

Heather, ĕrīca.

Heaven, caelum (not used in *pl*)

Heights, ardua (*n. pl.*) ; culmĭnă (*n. pl.*)

Help, ŏpem (*nom.* ops not used);
in *pl* = resources ; auxĭlium.
Hence, hĭnc.
Here, hīc.
Hereafter, posthac.
Hero, hērōs, -ōis ; vir.
Hill, collis ; hill - side, ridge,
jŭgum.
Hither, hūc ; hither and thither,
huc illuc.
Hoarse, raucus ; hoarse-sound-
ing, raucĭsŏnus.
Hold, to, těneo, -ere ; hold back,
rětĭneo.
Hollow, cǎvus ; the hollows, cava
(*n. p.*)
Holy, sǎcer, sǎcra, -um.
Home, dŏmus ; pěnātes (*lit.* house-
hold gods) ; at home, domi ;
(to) home, domum.
Honour, děcus, -ŏris ; honour-
able, ingěnuus ; hŏnestus.
Hope, spēs (spei not found),
spem.
Hour, hōra.
House, domus ; aedes (*pl.*) ; to
house = to store up, condo,
-ere.
Hover, vŏlĭto ; hover round,
circumvolito, -are.
How, quam.
Husband, conjux, -ŭgis; mǎrītus.
Hushed, to be, contĭcesco, -ere.

Idle, vānus ; ĭnānis ; ĭnūtĭlis.
If, sī ; if not, nĭ, nĭsĭ ; but if,
sĭn.
Ill, *adv.* mǎlĕ.
Ill-fated, infēlix, infaustus.
Illustrious, clārus.

Impaired, těměrātus ; not im-
paired, intemeratus.
Indian, Indus.
Infant, ĭnfans, -ntis.
Intelligence, mens.
Intervene, to, intercĭdo, -ere.
Invoke, testor, -ari.
Italian, Ĭtǎlus.
Ivy, hěděra.

Jest, jŏcus.
Join, jungo, -ere.
Journey, vĭa ; ĭter, ĭtĭněris.
Joy, laetĭtĭa.
Joyful, laetus.

Kiss, oscŭlum.
Knee, gěnū.
Know, to, nōvi, -isse (by acquaint-
ance) ; scio, -ire (by mental
faculties).
Known, nōtus.

Labour, lǎbor, -ōris.
Laid, condĭtus.
Land, terra ; tellus, -ūris ; native
land, pǎtria ; terra pǎterna.
Last, extrēmus, ultĭmus, sǔprē-
mus.
Lately, nūper ; too late, sēro
(*adv*), sērus (*adj.*)
Laugh, to, rideo, -ere ; laughter,
risus.
Lay, to, pŏno, -ere ; lay aside,
dēpōno ; lay down, pono ; de-
pono ; lay low, sterno, -ere.
Leaf, fŏlium ; cŏma ; frons, fron-
dis.
Leap, to, sǎlio, -ire.
Learn, to, disco, -ere, dĭdĭci.

Leave, to, linquo, rĕlinquo, -ĕre.

Length, at, tandem.

Less, mĭnor, -ōris ; (*adv.*) mĭnŭs.

Lie, to, jăceo, -ere ; rĕcŭbo, -are ;
to lie hid, lăteo, -ere.

Life, vita.

Light, lux, lūcis ; lūmen, -ĭnis.

Light (*adj.*), lĕvis.

Like, sĭmĭlis, with *gen.* or *dat. ;*
the former of inward, the latter
of outward, resemblance ; =
such as is, qualis ; instar, pār
(both with *gen.*)

Limb, membrum.

Line, ordo, -ĭnis.

Lip, labrum (ā generally).

Little, parvus, parvŭlus ; exĭguus.

Live, to, vīvo, -ere.

Living, vīvus.

Lock (of hair), căpillus, cŏma,
crinis.

Lofty, altus ; celsus.

Lonely, sŏlus.

Long, longus ; **for a long time,**
diu.

Look, vultus.

Look, to, compound of -spĭcĭo,
according to sense, as adspicio
(behold), despicio (look down
on), suspicio (look up to), pro-
spicio (look forth) ; respicio (look
back on, regard).

Loose, to, solvo, -ere ; **to let
loose,** effundo, -ere.

Lose, to, perdo, -ere.

Loss, damnum.

Lot, sors, sortis.

Love, ămor, -ŏris ; **a lover,**
ămans.

Love, to, ămo, -are.

Lowest, imus, infĭmus.

Lowly, hŭmĭlis.

Maid, maiden, puella ; virgo,
-ĭnis ; (*adj.*) puellāris ; vir-
gĭneus.

Make for = seek, repair to, pĕto,
-ere.

Man, hŏmŏ ; vĭr, vĭri (the former
= human being).

Manly, vĭrilis.

Many, multus ; **so many,** tŏt (indecl.) ; **very many** (oft. =
many), plūrĭmus.

Margin, margo, -ĭnis.

Mark, nŏta.

Marriage, conjŭgium.

Marvel, miror, -ari ; admiror,
-ari.

Mast, mālus.

Matters, it, rĕfert (*impers.*)

Medicine, mĕdĭcina, mĕdĭcāmen,
-ĭnis.

Meet together, to, cŏeo, -ire.

Mention, to make, mĕmŏro ; **to
be made mention of,** mĕmŏrā-
bĭlis.

Merchant, mercător, -ōris ; **mer-
chandise,** merces (*pl.*)

Merry, hĭlaris.

Mid, midst of, mĕdius.

Mind, mens (= understanding),
ănĭmus (= feelings).

Mindful, mĕmŏr, -ŏris (with
gen.)

Misfortune, mălum.

Moist, to be, mădeo, -ere.

Month, mensis.

Moon, lūna ; Cynthia.

Morn, morning, māne ; of-the-
morning (adj.), mātūtīnus.
Morrow, postĕra dies.
Mortal, mortalis.
Mother, māter, mātrıs ; gĕnĕtrix,
-īcis ; of a mother (adj.),
māternus.
Mound, tŭmŭlus.
Mountain, mons, montis ; of, or
on, the mountain (adj.), mon-
tānus.
Mournful, flēbĭlis ; maestus.
Murmur, murmur, -ŭris.
My, mine, meus. Sometimes
expressed by mihi, dat. of in-
direct object.
Myrtle, myrtus.

Name, nōmen, -ĭnis.
Native, păternus ; nātālis.
Native-place, pătria.
Nature, nātūra.
Neck, collum ; cervıx, -īcis.
Neglect, to, neglĕgo, -ere.
Nest, nīdus ; nestlings, nīdi
(pl.)
New, nŏvus.
Night, nox, noctis ; nightly,
nocturnus.
No, none, nullus ; no one, nemo,
with gen. and abl. borrowed
from nullus ; no other, some-
times non . . . alter ; no
longer, non jam ; non amplius.
Noble, nōbĭlıs ; gĕnĕrōsus.
None the less, non sēcius.
Not, nōn ; not yet, nondum.
Nothing, nought, nĭhĭl, nīl.
Now = at thıs time, nunc ; = by
this time, jam.

Nut, nux, nŭcis.
Nymph, nympha ; = maiden,
puella.

Obey, to, pāreo, -ere (with dat.)
Offspring, prōles ; sŏbŏles.
Often, saepĕ ; as often as, quo-
tiens ; so often, totiens.
Old (of persons), sĕnex ; oldest,
maximus natu ; (of thıngs),
antīquus ; vĕtus (=long estab-
lished).
On, in (abl.), sometimes only sign
of ablatıve.
Once, ōlim, quondam ; once for
all, sĕmel.
One, ūnus.
Only, tantum ; mŏdŏ ; sometimes
non nīsĭ.
Or (if you lıke), vel ; or else,
aut.
Order, ordo, -ĭnis.
Our, noster.
Outstretched, p.p. of tendo, or
extendo.
Outstrip, to, exsŭpĕro, -are.
Overwhelm, to, mergo, -ĕre.
Overshadow, ĭnumbro, -are.
Overturn, ēverto, subverto, -ere.
Own, suus.

Parent, părens ; (as an adj.),
păternus.
Pass, pass by, to, praetereo,
-ire.
Peace, pax, pācis.
People = a nation, pŏpŭlus ;
= persons, sunt qui ; hŏmĭnes.
Perform, ăgo, -ere.
Perhaps, fortasse ; forsĭtăn (subj.)

Perish, to, pĕreo, -ire.

Perjured, perjūrus; perjury, per-
jūrium.

Pestilential, pestĭférus.

Phœnician (*fem. adj.*), Phoenissa.

Piercing, ācūtus.

Pity, to, mĭsĕrĕor, -ēri (with
gen.)

Place, a, lŏcus ; (*pl.* loci = spots,
loca = regions).

Place, to, sisto, -ere.

Plaintive, quĕrŭlus.

Play, to, lūdo, -ere.

Pleasure, vŏluptas ; it is a pleasure, jŭvat.

Pledge, pignus, -oris ; foedus,
-ĕris.

Pluck, to, carpo, -ere.

Poplar, pōpŭlus

Pour, pour forth, fundo, -ere.

Praise, laus, laudis ; to praise,
laudo, -are.

Pray, to, ōro, -are.

Prayer, prĕcem (*acc.*), *nom. sing.*
not used ; *pl.* preces.

Precious, prĕtĭōsus.

Press, prĕmo, -ere.

Prize, praemium.

Prosperous, sĕcundus ; faustus ;
fortūnātus.

Prostrate, jăcens, -entis ; strātus.

Purpose, to no, nēquidquam,
incassum.

Put, pono, -ere ; put to, appono ;
suppono (of reaping) ; put
away, rĕmŏveo, -ere.

Quarrel, rixa.

Queen, rēgīna.

Quiet, plăcĭdus.

Quiver, to, trĕmo, -ere ; vĭbro,
-are.

Race, gens ; = lineage, gĕnus,
-ĕris ; = stock, stirps, stirpis.

Ray, jŭbăr, -ăris ; rădius.

Reaper, messor, -ōris.

Recall, rĕvŏco, -are ; = resemble,
rĕfĕro.

Recess, latĕbra ; rĕcessus.

Recline, rĕcŭbo, -are ; rĕcumbo,
-ere.

Recognise, agnosco, -ere, -ōvi,
-ĭtum.

Region, lŏcus; plăga; rĕgio, -ōnis.

Rejoice, to, laetor, -ari.

Rejoicing, laetĭtĭa.

Remain, to, măneo, -ere ; resto,

Remains, rĕlĭquĭae.

Remember, to, mĕmĭni, mĕmĭn-
isse , rĕmĭniscor, -i (*gen.*)

Renew, to, nŏvo, -are ; rĕnovo,
-are.

Renown, fāma.

Repair to, pĕto, -ĕre.

Repining, questus.

Repose, quies, -ētis ; rĕquies.

Resemble, to, rĕfĕro, -ferre (with
acc.)

Resolute, untiring, impĭger.

Resound, to, persŏno, -are ; rĕ-
sŏno.

Rest (*s.*), quies, -ētis ; rĕquies.

Rest, the, rĕlĭquus (*adj.*)

Return, rĕvertor, rĕdeo, -ire; = to
give back, reddo, -ere.

Revel, to, bacchor, -ari.

Right hand. See Hand.

Rigid, dūrus, rĭgĭdus.

Ripe, mātūrus.

Rise, ŏrior, ŏrīri ; surgo, -ere.

Rising, ortus.

Roam, to, văgor, -ari ; roam through, pĕrăgro, -are ; pĕrerro, -are.

Rock, saxum, rūpes.

Rocky, saxeus.

Roll, to, volvo, -ere.

Rose, rŏsa ; rosy, rŏseus.

Row, ordo, -ĭnis.

Ruddy, rŭber, rŭbra, -um.

Rugged, rūgōsus

Ruin, ruīna.

Ruin, to, perdo, -ere.

Rule, to, rĕgo, -ere.

Ruthless, saevus.

Sagacious, săgax, -ācis.

Sail, vēlum, carbăsum (in pl.), linteum (in pl.)

Sailor, nauta, nāvĭta.

Same, the, idem, ĕădem, ĭdem.

Sand, hărēna ; sandy, hărēnōsus.

Save = except, nĭsĭ (conj.), praeter (prep. with acc.)

Say, to, dīco, -ere ; says he (she, etc.), ăĭt.

Scanty, exĭguus.

Scarcely, vix, aegrē.

Scatter, to, spargo, -ĕre.

Sceptre, sceptrum.

Scour = to race over, lustro, -are.

Scud, to, vŏlĭto, -are; scud over, transvŏlĭto.

Scythian (adj.), Scȳthĭcus.

Sea, măre, măris ; pontus ; open sea, pelagus ; deep sea, altum, prŏfundum.

Season, tempestas, -ātis ; hōra.

Seat, sēdes.

Secluded, āvius.

Second (of two) alter ; sĕcundus.

See, to, vĭdeo, -ere.

See ! ēn ; eccĕ ; adspĭcĕ.

Seek, pĕto, -ere ; quaero, -ere.

Seem, to, vĭdeor, -eri, visus sum.

Seize, răpio, -ĕre ; arrĭpio.

Self, ipse ; thyself, tu . . . ipse, etc., or simply defined by person of verb.

Separate, to, disjungo, -ere ; dissŏcio, -are ; sēcerno, -ere.

Separated, discrētus.

Sepulchre, sĕpulcrum.

Shade, umbra ; tenĕbrae.

Shadow, umbra.

Shelter, to, tĕgo, -ere.

Shepherd, pastor, -ōris.

Shine, to, nĭteo, -ere ; shining, candens.

Ship, nāvis.

Shoot up, to, exsĭlio, -ire.

Shore, lītus, -ōris ; ōra.

Short, short-lived, brĕvis.

Shout, to raise a, conclāmo, -are.

Shower, imber, -ris.

Sickle, falx, falcis.

Sigh, to, suspiro, -are; ingĕmo, -ere.

Sign, signal, signum.

Sink down, to, prŏcumbo, -ere.

Silence, sĭlentium (pl.)

Silent, sĭlens, -entis.

Simple, simplex, -ĭcis.

Single, ūnus.

Sit, to, sĕdeo, -ere.

Skill, sollertia.

Skim, to, rādo, -ĕre.

Slaughter, caedes.

Slay, caedo, -ere ; occido.

Sleep, somnus ; deep sleep, sŏpor, ōris.

Slumber, sopor, -ōris.

Slumbering, sōpitus.

Smile, risus.

Smile, to, subrideo, -ere.

Smite down, or off, dēcŭtio, -ĕre.

Snatch, to, răpio, -ĕre ; snatch away, ābrĭpio

So (in comparison), sic ; ĭtă ; non ălĭter , haud alĭter.

So = to such a degree, ădeō.

Soil, sŏlum ; tellus, ūris.

Solace, sōlāmen, -ĭnis ; sōlatium (pl.)

Soldier, miles, -ĭtis.

Song, cantus ; carmen, -ĭnis.

Soon, mox ; as soon as, sĭmŭl ac.

Soothe, to, lēnio, -ire ; sēdo, -are.

Sorrowful, maestus.

Sound, sŏnus, sonĭtus.

Sound, to, sŏno, -are ; rĕsono.

Source, fons, fontis.

Spanish, Hispānus.

Sparkle, to, mĭco, -are.

Spirit, spiritus , = courage, ănĭmus.

Splendid, ēgrĕgius.

Spontaneously, spontĕ.

Spot, lŏcus. See Place.

Spouse, conjux, -ŭgis.

Spread, to, pando, -ere.

Spring, vēr, vēris ; of spring, vernus.

Stand, to, sto, -are ; to take one's stand on, insisto, -ere

(dat.) ; to stand round, circumsto, -are ; stand by, adsto (dat.)

Standard, signum ; vexillum.

Star (a single) stella ; = constellation, sidus, -ĕris ; starry, astrĭfer, -ĕra ; sīdĕreus.

Start, to. See Advance.

Stay, to, sisto -ĕre (trans.) ; măneo, -ere (intrans.)

Steadfast, firmus ; constans.

Step, passus ; gressus ; pēs, pĕdis.

Stiff, to be, torpeo, -ere.

Stir, to, ăgĭto, -are (= disturb) ; cieo, -ere (= rouse).

Stores, ŏpes, ŏpum (pl.)

Storm, hiems, hiemis ; prŏcella ; tempestas, -ātis ; storm-cloud, nimbus.

Strain, carmen, -ĭnis ; mŏdi (pl.)

Stream, amnis ; (a small) rīvus.

Stream, to, fluĭto, -are.

Streaming, effūsus.

Strength, vires (pl. of vīs) ; rōbur, -ŏris.

Strew, to, spargo, -ere.

Strong, fortis.

Such, tālis.

Sudden, sŭbĭtus ; suddenly, sŭbĭto ; on a sudden, rĕpentĕ.

Suit, to, convĕnio, -ire (with dat.)

Suitor, prŏcus.

Summer, aestas, -ātis ; of summer (adj.), aestivus.

Summit of, summus, agreeing with noun.

Sun, sōl, sōlis.

Supply, to, suppĕdĭto, -are.

Support, fulcio, -ire.

Suppress, to, supprĭmo, -ere.

Sweep off, to, dēcutio, -ĕre.

Sweet, dulcis ; suavis : the former the word for saccharine sweetness. 'Tis sweet, jŭvat (impers.)

Swell, to, turgeo, -ere ; tŭmesco.

Swift, răpĭdus ; swifter, ōcior.

Sword, ensis ; glădius.

Take, accipio, -ere ; take away (of blessings) ădĭmo ; (of bad things) exĭmo, -ere.

Teach, dŏceo, -ere ; ēdŏceo.

Tear, lăcrĭma.

Tell of, mĕmŏro, -are ; narro, -are.

Tempest. See Storm.

Tempestuous, nimbōsus.

Tender, tĕnĕr.

Than, quam. Also sign of abl. after comp.

That = in order that, ut (subj.) ; that . . . not, ne (subj.)

That (of yours) iste, also with contemptuous force ; that yonder, ille.

Then, tum, tunc ; = after that, inde ; = therefore, ĭgĭtur.

There, ĭbĭ ; illĭc.

Third, tertius.

This (here), hĭc.

Thou, tū, tĕ, tuī, tĭbī.

Though, lĭcet (with subj.), quamvis (subj.), quanquam (ind)

Thousand, millē (indecl)

Thread, filum.

Threshold, limen, -ĭnis.

Throb, to, mĭco, -are, micuı.

Throng, a, turba ; căterva.

Throng round, to, circumfundor, -i.

Through, per (acc.)

Thus, sic.

Tide, aestus.

Time, tempus, -ŏris ; at times, quondam, saepe ; if at times, si quando.

Together, ūnā ; sĭmŭl ; părĭtĕr.

Too, nĭmĭs, nimium. Also sign of comp. degree.

Top, culmen, -ĭnis ; fastigium.

Topmost, top of the, summus (agr. with noun).

Touch, to, tango, -ere.

Trace, vestigium.

Trailing, pensĭlia.

Tranquil, plăcĭdus ; tranquillus.

Traverse, to, pĕrăgro, -are ; lustro, -are.

Treacherous, fallax, -ācis.

Treasure, ŏpes (pl.)

Tremble, to, trĕmo, -ere.

True, vērus ; the truth, vērum.

Trustful, crēdŭlus.

Tune, to, mŏdŭlor, -ari.

Turf, caespĕs, -ĭtis.

Turns, by, vĭcĭbus ; inque vicem.

Two, duŏ, duŏrum.

Unceasing, perpĕtuus.

Uncertain, incertus, dŭbius.

Undying, aeternus.

Unequal, impăr, -ăris.

Unhappy, infēlix ; infaustus, mĭser.

Unharmed, sine fraude.

Unite, to, sŏcio, -are ; united, sŏcius.

Unwept, indēflētus.

Unwonted, insŏlĭtus.

Upbear, sustĭneo, -ere

O

Uplift, to, tollo, -ere, sustŭli, sublātum.

Upper, sŭpĕrus.

Use, to, ūtor, uti, usus.

Used to, often a sign of the *imperf.* tense. See also accustomed.

Utter, to, dico, -ere ; sometimes by such phrases as vōce ciēre.

Vain, vānus, inūtĭlis ; in vain, frustrā.

Vale, valley, vallis.

Vanish, to, vānesco, -ere.

Vernal, vernus.

Verse, versus.

Villager, pāgānus.

Vine, vitis.

Visible, spectābĭlis.

Voice, vox, vōcis.

Vow, vōtum.

Wall, mūrus (general term) ; moenia (*pl.*) = fortified walls ; paries, pariĕtĭs (scanned parjetis) = a house wall.

Wander, to, erro, -are ; văgor, -ari ; pălor, -ari (= straggle).

War, bellum ; mars, martis.

Warning, mŏnĭtus.

Warrior, bellātor, -ōris.

Watch = behold, specto, -are ; = keep watch, vĭgĭlo, -are.

Water, ăqua. For waters (of the sea) various words may be used, as aequora, marmora, frēta (all *pl.*) ; gurgĕs, -ĭtis.

Wave, unda ; fluctus.

Wave, to (in the wind), ventĭlo, are; = toss, jacto, -are.

Way, via ; wayfarer, vĭātor, -ōris.

Wealth, ŏpes (*pl.*), divĭtiae (*pl.*)

Weapon, tēlum.

Weary, fessus, lassus, fătĭgātus.

Weave, necto, -ere ; texo, -ere ; contexo.

Weep, to, fleo, -ēre ; dēfleo.

Weeping, flētus.

Well, bĕnĕ.

Well out, to, exundo, -are.

Whale, bālaena.

When, cum ; when ? quando.

Whence, unde.

Where, qua, ūbi.

White, albus ; (glistening white), candĭdus.

Whitening, albens ; albescens ; canescens (of ripe grain).

Whither, quo.

Who, qui ; Who ? quis.

Wide, lātus ; widely, late.

Wife, conjux, uxor.

Willow, sălix, -ĭcis.

Win, to, = gain, părio, -ĕre ; = to conquer, vinco, -ere.

Wind, ventus. Special names of winds often to be preferred, as Bŏrĕas (N.), Eurus (E.), Nŏtus (S), Zĕphȳrus (W.)

Winter, hiemps, hĭĕmis ; wintry, hiĕmālia.

Wise, săpiens, -ntis.

Wise, in such. See So.

Wish, to, vŏlo, velle, vŏlui.

Without, sĭnĕ.

Woe = misfortune, mălum ; = sorrow, maeror ; maestitia.

Wood, silva ; nĕmus ; woodlands, saltus (*pl.*)

VOCABULARY.

Word, verbum ; vox, vŏcis.
Would that ! ŭtĭnam ; o utinam ;
  o si (all with *subj.*)
Wound, vulnus, -ĕris; to wound,
  lăcĕro, -are ; vulnĕro, -are.
Wrap, to, tĕgo, -ere.
Write, to, scribo, -ere.

Year, annus.

Yesterday, hĕri.
Yet = nevertheless, tămeı
  (of time), ădhūc.
Yield, to, cēdo, -ere.
Young, jŭvĕnilis ; the
  jŭvĕnes.
Youth, a, jŭvĕnis, puer.
Youth, time of, jŭventa; jı
  -ūtis.

THE END.

Printed by R. & R. CLARK, *Edinburgh.*

BIBLIOLIFE

Old Books Deserve a New Life
www.bibliolife.com

Did you know that you can get most of our titles in our trademark **EasyScript**™
print format? **EasyScript**™ provides readers with a larger than average
typeface, for a reading experience that's easier on the eyes.

Did you know that we have an ever-growing collection of books in
many languages?

Order online:
www.bibliolife.com/store

Or to exclusively browse our **EasyScript**™ collection:
www.bibliogrande.com

At BiblioLife, we aim to make knowledge more accessible by
making thousands of titles available to you – quickly and affordably.

Contact us:
BiblioLife
PO Box 21206
Charleston, SC 29413

CPSIA information can be obtained at www.ICGtesting.com
Printed in the USA
BVOW021938131112

305441BV00013BA/23/A